THE ATHABASCA RYGA

THE ATHABASCA RYGA

George Ryga

Edited by E. David Gregory

Talonbooks   •   Vancouver   •   1990

published with the assistance of The Canada Council and the Athabasca University

Talonbooks
201/1019 East Cordova Street
Vancouver, British Columbia
Canada, V6A 1M8

Typeset in Century by Pièce de Résistance Ltée. Printed and bound in Canada by Hignell Printing.

Some of these works were originally broadcast on the CBC and produced by CBC TV, "Notes from a Silent Boyhood" was published in *Clover and Wild Strawberries: A History of the Schools of the Country of Athabasca.*

"The Pitchfork" was published in *Beyond a Crimson Morning* (Doubleday Canada).

Rights to produce "Village Crossroad" and/or "Storm," in whole or in part, in any medium by any group, amateur or professional, are retained by George Ryga & Associates Inc. Interested persons are requested to write: P.O. Box 430, Summerland, B.C., Canada, V0H 1Z0.

First printing: June 1990

Canadian Cataloguing in Publication Data

Ryga, George, 1932-
 Athabasca Ryga

 ISBN 0-88922-276-2

 I. Gregory, David. II. Title.
PS8585.Y5A8 1990   C818'.5409   C90-091305-3
PR9199.3.R93A8 1990

*For George's
mother, father, sister:
Mary, George, Ann*

CONTENTS

PREFACE

I never had the good fortune to meet George Ryga, and I was slow to discover his writings. Soon after I made my home in Canada, in 1969, I heard talk of an interesting and controversial play, *The Ecstasy of Rita Joe*, but I found no opportunity to see it, and quickly forgot the author's name. Fifteen years later the university where I teach, Athabasca University, was uprooted from Edmonton and transplanted to the small town of Athabasca, some one hundred and fifty kilometers north. My family and I chose to relocate with the university, and it only took a few months of living there for me to realize I had landed in a strange but interesting place. I joined the local historical society, and started finding out more about the colourful past of the town and the region. I even ended up writing a book: *Athabasca Landing: An Illustrated History*, which was published in 1986. As part of my search for information I read two novels which the municipal librarian informed me were set in the Athabasca area and written by a famous Canadian writer who had grown up on a farm north of town.

The novels were *Hungry Hills* and *Ballad of a Stonepicker*, and they proved to be the best things I ever found that captured in words the feel, the atmosphere, the touch and smell of rural Athabasca, and, moreover, helped to explain the values, attitudes, and lifestyles of the older inhabitants of the area. George Ryga, of course, was the "famous Canadian writer," and I was hooked. Over the next couple of years I gradually explored all the books — novels and plays — by him in the

9

local library, and encouraged both the university and municipal libraries to purchase anything in print that they were missing. After reading such other novels as *Night Desk* and *In the Shadow of the Vulture*, and such plays as *Indian, The Ecstasy of Rita Joe*, "Grass and Wild Strawberries," *Captives of the Faceless Drummer, Sunrise on Sarah*, "Paracelsus", and *A Letter to My Son*, I became convinced that here indeed was a major Canadian talent, a writer of international importance. Why, then, had I not heard of George Ryga before? And why did there seem to be so little awareness and interest in his work among Athabascans, either in the local or the university community?

In the local Ukrainian community I found much indifference and even some hostility to a native son who was perceived to have left home and gotten involved with the wrong sort of politics. But there were exceptions: George Ryga did have some fervent fans in Athabasca, most notably Nick and Nettie Evasiuk who had kept in touch with him and had done their best to collect copies of everything he had published. Nick, it transpired, had even written to the university suggesting Ryga should be considered for an honourary doctorate, but the idea had gone nowhere. I thought it was an eminently reasonable idea, and determined to make a second attempt. Knowing that university committees are impressed by thick sheaves of paper, I gathered together as much information as I could find on Ryga's career and writings, and, with the help of the library staff, compiled a mini-dossier of reviews, favourable and not-so-favourable (Ryga was a controversial author, no question about it). In the process I discovered that Dr. Jim Hoffman of East Kootenay College, Cranbrook, B.C., was writing a biography of George Ryga, and he generously shared with me data that he had collected. I also learned that Ryga had sold most of his personal archives, including many manuscripts, to the University of Calgary. When I visited Calgary I found among those manuscripts several early, unpublished, works — short stories, plays, and even two full-length novels — dating from Ryga's Alberta years and relating, directly or indirectly, to Athabasca.

My materials supporting the nomination of George Ryga as Honourary Doctor of Athabasca University were complete, and Nick and I were drafting the covering letter, when we heard the sad news: George Ryga had died of stomach cancer at the age of fifty-five. That ruled out the honourary doctorate (which cannot be awarded posthumously) but the university decided to go ahead and commemorate Athabasca's most famous author at its June 1988 convocation, during which a plaque was unveiled in George Ryga's memory by his daughter, the actress Tanya Ryga. It may now be seen in the main entrance lobby of the university, and incorporates the following quotation from Ryga's play "Paracelsus":

To you I bequeath this sword . . . and the most fearful
legacy of all, the curse of continual enquiry . . .
plus my eternal love to lift you to the lip of
heaven, while still you pace and prod this earth
for what truth and honesty still unknown lies
buried in the herbs, stones and essences like a
mantel of the gods . . . waiting to redress human pain
and want.

This seems a fitting memorial to a writer who never rested in his search for truth, no matter how unpopular that honest and unremitting enquiry made him in some circles. Yet the best way of honouring a writer is to publish him, and George Ryga left behind several manuscripts that were close enough to completion to warrant publication. The university (in the persons of President Terry Morrison and Vice-President Academic Ross Paul) therefore encouraged me to do what I could to ensure that some more of George Ryga's early writings about Athabasca and the Athabasca region would find their way into print. This book is the result. One of the chief aims of *The Athabasca Ryga* is to illustrate, as far as possible in George Ryga's own words, his ethnic and cultural background and the geographical setting in which he had his roots.

The book would not exist without the blessing and co-operation of Norma Ryga and Keith Ledbury (of George Ryga

& Associates Inc.) and Karl Siegler of Talonbooks who have shared my enthusiasm for the project, notwithstanding our occasional fierce disagreements over the precise contents of the volume. As a historian and resident of Athabasca, I had one conception of the book. Karl, as a publisher and experienced editor who had often worked with George Ryga, had another. Keith, as the guardian of George's literary reputation, had a third. After much use of various telecommunication services between Alberta and British Columbia we came to a compromise. It is, I believe, a good compromise. We could not include all of George's extant and unpublished early manuscripts, but *The Athabasca Ryga* provides a fine selection from the best of them. Any student of George Ryga's work who has time (and financing) to spend several days in the University of Calgary archives will, no doubt, discover other treasures there that may, some day, also find their way into print. In the meantime, I trust all of George Ryga's admirers will find much to enjoy in this volume. My hope is that it will also help to consolidate and enhance his growing reputation as a writer of international stature. I would like to express my sincere gratitude to Keith Ledbury, who has provided me with an enormous amount of assistance throughout the two-year task of compiling and refining this book. His meticulous and timely attention to the various stages of the manuscript which arrived at his doorstep have helped create a book that I'm sure Ryga would be pleased with. I would also like to take this opportunity to express my appreciation for the aid and advice given me by Jim Hoffman and by my wife Rosaleen, and for the information provided by Norma Ryga and by several members of the Ukrainian community in Athabasca. The following introduction to this collection of George Ryga's Athabasca writings would be the poorer without their help. Needless to say they are not responsible for any errors or omissions it may yet contain.

E. David Gregory
Humanities Department
Athabasca University

INTRODUCTION

THE PIONEER HERITAGE

Drop a pebble into a pool of water and ripples spread out in concentric circles from the point of impact. George Ryga's early life resembled the rippled surface of that disturbed pool. He moved by stages away from his place of origin, but the focus of his existence remained his childhood home, a pioneer homestead near Deep Creek in Northern Alberta. As he began to grow up, he encountered, beyond his family circle, the neighbouring farmers, their children, and the one-room schoolhouse that served the Richmond Park area in which Deep Creek was situated. His teens took him a step further away, to the neighbouring small town of Athabasca, some thirty-five kilometers to the south-west, with its grain elevators, cafes, stores, bank, hotel, lumber yards, and occasional chautauqua or circus. Further yet were the logging camps of the boreal forest, a mainstay of the local economy. And from one hundred and fifty kilometers further south came the siren call of the city, a harsh and hostile world that yet held out the promise of employment and, perhaps, experiences unknown in the rural north. Beyond Edmonton stretched the highways: west over the Rockies to the warmer climate of the Okanagan and to the coastal rainforests, east across the prairies to the fascinations of other landscapes and the cities of central Canada, especially Toronto and Montreal. Further yet, across the Atlantic Ocean, lay the land of his family's roots, the south-west Ukraine, and the home of his adopted language, Great Britain.

George Ryga settled permanently in Summerland, B.C., in 1963. Before then, his early life in Alberta was an exploration, a restless quest that took him further and further from that epicentre near Deep Creek. Yet he never forgot his origins, and much of his early writing was, directly or indirectly, about the family farm, Richmond Park, Athabasca, and Edmonton. One of the main goals of this selection from his youthful manuscripts and later retrospective writings about the Athabasca region is to document this staunchly Canadian author's ambivalent relationship to his geographical and cultural place of origin.

Brought into the world by a rural midwife on July 27th, 1932, and named after his father, the young George grew up as a farm-boy, speaking his parents' tongue, Ukrainian. The family homestead was situated on a quarter-section of land near the north-west bank of the Athabasca River, some thirty-five kilometers north-east of the small town of Athabasca. Officially, the region was called Richmond Park, a rather incongruous name for an area settled predominantly by immigrants from Scandinavia and Eastern Europe. Deep Creek was a local name, a name derived from the small stream that flowed down a steep ravine to empty into the Athabasca River. The scattered community was mainly Ukrainian, but as George began to grow up he encountered, beyond the immediate family circle, neighbours who were Polish, German, Russian, Scottish, and Icelandic.[1]

George's own parents had come to Alberta from the part of the Ukraine near the Carpathian Mountains that was then (in the decades between the two World Wars) south-eastern Poland. They had been economic refugees, seeking a better life in a new land. Richmond Park had lured them with its promise of virgin land, still available to pioneers who would pay $10, build a homestead, clear the bush or forest, and begin farming the soil. The Rygas were late pioneers. Most of the Athabasca region had been settled in the decade before the First World War, but there were two good reasons why Richmond Park had not. For a start, communications were poor. To get there you had to cross the Athabasca River, but there was no bridge, just a small ferry in summer, an ice-road in winter, and a rather terrifying cable-car in spring and fall, after which you faced a day's drive through mud, dust, or snow (depending on the season) to get to virgin bush and forest. Then, as the Rygas and their neighbours quickly found out, the soil beneath the natural vegetation was a sticky, heavy clay. Not impossible farming soil, but not the best by any stretch of the imagination, just the best that was available at a price they could afford. So they stuck it out, or at least some of them did. But in the dirty thirties, times were hard, and the pioneer life was a struggle. As George recalled some forty years later in an interview with Peter Hay, "It was very primitive; in essence life hadn't changed from what it was in the 17th century in Eastern Europe . . . a lot of the impressions of how people live when reduced to bare essentials still persist in my mind . . . My father didn't know when the thirties ended and the good times began . . . He worked this farm for thirty-two years. The value of this farm, with all equipment and the farmhouse, at the time of his retirement, was $8,000 . . ."[2]

George Ryga sen. hailed from the village of Sivka, near Kalush. In 1927, when he was in his mid-twenties his exasperation with the backward, neo-feudal conditions of life in Pilsudski's authoritarian and nationalist Polish state had driven him to buy a boat passage to Canada. In 1930 he had married Mary Kolodka, the adopted daughter of another immigrant family from the Polish Ukraine, the Pidzarkos, who had also settled in Deep Creek. George jun. was their first born; a younger sister, Ann, followed in 1935.[3] When their parents arrived in Richmond Park the community had no school, but by the time young George reached the age of six it boasted a one-room log school, thanks in part to the efforts of the Rygas who were anxious that their children should have opportunities in Canada that had been hard to come by in Poland. Mary Ryga's knowledge of reading, writing and simple mathematics were restricted to what she needed for practical tasks around the farm and kitchen. Her son later recalled that these limited accomplishments did not come easy to her: "My mother . . . learnt to write her name, learnt to count up the number of bushels the farm was producing . . . it wasn't a welcome skill, it was a very difficult thing and they all resisted it . . . My father didn't. I must say this, he did not because he had at least a basic education in the old country . . ."[4]

George sen., indeed, was one of the better-educated members of the local Ukrainian community. He read pretty much everything in his native language that he could get his hands on, from Taras Shevchenko and Nikolai Gogol to agricultural and political magazines. In this he was unusual; and there were other ways, too, in which he was not typical of his neighbours. One was his politics: he was a socialist who hated Pilsudski's regime in Poland much more than Stalin's in the USSR, a point of view which did not endear him to some of his fellow settlers. Another was his religion, or rather lack of it. In spiritual terms Richmond Park was split five ways, between Anglicans, Lutherans (mainly the Germans and Icelanders), Roman Catholics (the Poles and a few of the Ukrainians), Ukrainian Catholics, and members of the Ukrainian Greek Orthodox Church. George Ryga sen., however, had little time for any of these varieties of Christianity, and wasn't reticent about showing his scepticism, either. His aggressive atheism often led to conflicts with pious neighbours who regarded him as a hardened reprobate. One such incident stuck in the mind of the young George, who recreated it in his travel memoir, *Beyond the Crimson Morning*, written in the wake of an extended visit to Communist China:

> A hot day in a summer of my boyhood. We were
> returning from town, my father and I, in greasy
> overalls and an old Essex car with defective steering.

A cloud of dust approached on the country road, lifted by a farm truck with a state box and three people peering out from behind a coated windshield. We pulled over and stopped, for once the truck passed us visibility was bad until the dust settled. Pulling along side of us, the truck also stopped. The dust it agitated and the dust following our car met and swirled around our vehicles for the duration of our pleasantries.

"Hello, Bill," my father greeted our neighbour four farms to the west of us.

"Hullo . . . Seen any hail in town?"

"Nope. Why do you ask?"

"There's been a dark cloud hanging across the river since noon. With this heat, a shift in the wind an' she's down over us," our neighbour announced and spat a stream of tobacco in the direction of our car door on my father's side. I didn't hear it hit the door, but I could smell its pungent odor over the alkali scent of dust.

"Who's with you in the truck?" my father asked.

"Wife an' the girl . . . we're goin' to church."

"What for? This is Tuesday."

"Won't hurt to pray a little for that cloud to go aroun' my place, in case it's carrying hail. I got a good stand of wheat headed out an' bloomin' right now. Don't want to lose it."

A grin spread over my father's stubble-bearded face. A malicious, trouble-making grin. "You remember the legal land description of your farm? Seems to me you're always confused about that."

"What for do I have to know that?" The dust was settling and I saw a scowl come over our neighbour's face as he stared at my father.

"Well, when you're praying you should maybe recite your legal land description so God knows what he's supposed to avoid with His thunder. Would be a waste of praying to do all that and give the wrong location . . .

17

you'd save someone else's crop and lose your own!''

The neighbour's wife, who always smelled of wet dog and shouted, even when she spoke in a small room, now leaned toward my father, her eyes narrowed and shining with anger.

"Drive to the church!" she hollered in her husband's ear, then pointed a thick finger at my father. "And you! I'm gonna pray so the hail comes an' hits you — right in your barley field! Maybe kill a couple of chickens, too! . . . An' cut your cabbage to manure!''

The neighbour spat again, and this time he did hit our car door. I could hear the splat. He then ground his gears and lurched the truck forward, the stake box in the back rattling and creaking as he drove by to his prayers. For a long moment my father sat, staring ahead, still grinning. Then he eased the car into gear, and with both hands on the wheel, jarred it back on the road and in the direction of home.

"Son," he said, "the sonsofbitches are okay . . . it's the others you've got to watch.''

And he began singing a happy folk song, as if he didn't have a worry in the world.[5]

The young George's mother, Mary, did not share her husband's scepticism. She was a practicing Ukrainian Catholic, and she did her best to see that her son was raised in the faith, taking him to church when she had the opportunity, and receiving occasional visits from itinerant priests. Apparently she had good reason to believe that these seeds were not falling on stony ground since the boy was sensitive to the wonders and mysteries of the natural world and, moreover, was blessed with an unusually spiritual disposition at an early age. Indeed, according to his own rather hyperbolic testimony, the young Ryga at the age of six "reached a higher elevation of religious sensitivity and revelation than any adult human I have since spoken to.''[6] The child initially had no way of expressing this mystical bent — it would later reappear as one facet of his style as a writer — but his youthful religiosity was noticed by mother and clergy, and before he reached his teens he had been singled out as a potential candidate for religious orders. In the summer of 1943 he attended a month-long retreat at a Catholic mission school near Athabasca, one of the childhood experiences that stood out in his mind when he drew upon his memories of Deep Creek and Athabasca to write the beginning segment of an unfinished and unpublished quasi-autobiographical novel, "The Bridge," in 1959-60. In the end, George Ryga, like his father, rebelled against formal religion, and his career was to be that of a writer not a priest. But he was not unmarked by his early instruction in the ideas and values of the Christian gospels, and in later life he treasured his youthful religious revelations as he treasured his other memories of life on the farm near Deep Creek.

CHILDHOOD ON THE FARM

The experience of growing up on a farm remained of fundamental importance to George Ryga throughout his life. He recognized this in correspondence he had in the late '60s with a young Edmonton schoolgirl, Zoë Cope, who had sent him a questionnaire seeking information about his early life and its impact on his literary work. Ryga replied: "My childhood in its entirety is one outstanding memory. Even today, when I am very far past childhood, the taste of saskatoons and wild strawberries is still fresh in my mouth, and I remember faces and gestures and neighbours' stories as if they were told me only an hour ago. Yet many of these voices have long been stilled by death, and the countryside and its buildings from which I emerged changed beyond recognition. But if I was to rebuild from recollection, I could do it with fine accuracy. Yes, it all affects my life. Over my fireplace in Summerland still hang parts of an iron harness like the one I used to strap around the collars of my father's farm horses. I still wake to the bark of a dog, happily, for we had dogs then. I never leave food on a plate, for often food was scarce when I was a child, and to sit down to dinner was a sacred obligation.''[7]

Even his first published writing, ''Smoke,'' an essay he composed in 1949 when aged seventeen, describes, with straightforward and accurate first-hand knowledge, the everyday lives of the Ukrainian homesteaders, their sacrifices, their achievements, and their dogged pioneer spirit. One cannot read the essay without acquiring a real feeling for what it was like to farm a quarter-section in Richmond Park in the 1930s. It remains the best single source we have for comprehending the geographical setting and the historical context in which Ryga grew up.

In his early twenties, before he had found his mature voice as a writer, Ryga wrote a considerable amount of poetry, some of which was published in 1956 in the collection *Song of My Hands*. Pastoral verses such as ''Summer Rain'' and ''Twilight,'' which evoke the countryside around the family homestead, are evidence of the young man's feeling for and appreciation of the natural environment of Deep Creek and, more generally, the Athabasca region. ''My Land'' is a celebration of the pioneer farmer, his land, his toil in making it productive, and his success in bringing forth fields of golden grain. ''Song of the Farmer'' and ''The Neighbouring Farmer'' demonstrate Ryga's sympathy and respect for men like his father, the pioneers who struggled against adverse climatic and economic conditions to keep their family farms viable. Their achievements were substantial, and they obtained a measure of satisfaction from them, yet, as the farm boy knew from personal experience, their lives were hard, and the material rewards they received from their never-ending work hardly raised them above the poverty level.

When he first began seriously writing for a living in the early '60s, George Ryga's profusion of manuscripts showed beyond a shadow of a doubt that he had an eye for noticing, a mind for remembering, and a gift for recreating in words incidents and details from his everyday experiences as a child. The opening sequence of ''The Bridge,'' drafted in 1959-60, was but the first occasion on which this talent was put to good use. An unpublished collection of ten short stories and a play, written between 1960 and 1962 and collectively titled "Poor People," also drew directly on the young author's recollections of the lives and idiosyncracies of the neighbouring farming folk. So too did Ryga's first two published novels, *Hungry Hills* (1963) and *Ballad of a Stone-Picker* (1966). Indeed, the majority of his early work was constructed from the more unusual and striking scenes of Richmond Park life. They demonstrate the young Ryga's sympathetic feeling for the sometimes-strange characters of his local community, but they also reveal his psychological distance from them. He loved them, after a fashion, but from the beginning he observed them with a detached and ironic eye.

Two of the plays for which George Ryga is most famous, *Indian* (1962), and *The Ecstasy of Rita Joe* (1967) derive in spirit and texture from his youthful personal knowledge of and friendships with the Treaty Indians and Métis of the Calling Lake region north-west of Richmond Park. And Ryga's little-known essay, "Notes from a Silent Boyhood" (which was first published in *Clover and Wild Strawberries*, a historical survey of the one-room log schools of the Athabasca area), is a charming yet incisive reflection on the lessons and meaning of the years 1932-1945 and their impact on his later intellectual development. Furthermore, one of Ryga's best later plays, *A Letter to My Son* (1981), portrays an old Ukrainian farmer, not unlike George Ryga sen., trying to communicate with his son who, like George Ryga jun., has left the farm to pursue a different kind of life. Asked by the CBC to give a short radio talk, Ryga wrote "Essay on *A Letter to My Son*," an intense and revealing account of what it meant to grow up as a member of an ethnic minority in Alberta in the 1940s. This essay, however, focussed on Ryga's teenage perceptions of his rural Ukrainian community and its relations with the surrounding Anglo-Saxon world, a subject to which we shall return later.

A few years earlier, when writing an account of his experiences travelling in Communist China in 1976, Ryga found his mind flashing back to earlier, parallel incidents in his life, including scenes from his childhood. Some of these memories he incorporated in the published memoir of this expedition, *Beyond the Crimson Morning*. An incident that stuck in the young farmboy's mind involved his father and another neighbour, and, at least for the mature writer, came to possess a symbolic value. As Ryga recalled it the scene was as follows:

> When I was a boy, a neighbour on a nearby farm, a ferocious drunkard, was going through a second season of madness. One day in the heat of summer he was on the edge of his field, stripped to his trousers, attacking a forest of trees with an axe in his hands. One by one, the poplar trees fell before him, their leafy branches groaning. Soaked in his own perspiration, gasping for breath, his eyes wild, face contorted with rage and pain, the man worked as one possessed. "Why does he work like that? He is not starving, so why does he need more land so desperately?" I asked my father. "No. His needs are more fearful." "What are his needs?" I asked again. "He is wrestling with the devil, my boy. Leave him alone . . . leave him to do what he must do." "But will he win?" I wanted to know, not yet understanding the awesome struggle of this neighbour, for I was only a boy. "No," my father replied, his own eyes now agitated. "But he cannot surrender, or he would destroy us all . . ." Now the man is buried under the earth that gave him no rest. My father is an ancient man, still searching the hillsides through dimming sight for truth that has eluded him all these years. And I, and those nearest me, prowl through the climates, languages, and terrains of the world for similar reasons, a defiant eagle peering over my shoulders, its claws deeply embedded in my back.[8]

The symbolic importance of such childhood memories is examined in detail later in this introduction.

THE TEENAGE YEARS

Ryga wrote in "Notes from a Silent Boyhood" that before he went to school his world consisted mainly of what he could touch, taste, smell: "Rubber footwear mouldering in the sun, sour mud after a northern rain, the touch of newly turned earth, the acid scent of poplar leaves and the steel-coldness of winters whose presence was felt for the greater part of each year. Bread baking and split wood, sweating horses, smoke and kerosene, clover and wild strawberries — the coarse touch of tamarack wood, cruel as the arguments of cursing men who were always on the edge of violence, for the poverty was incredible and patience an unpredictable pool of water over which a storm always threatened . . . I could neither read nor write. I was silent and alone, for every sensation and experience was my own with no influence or direction . . . ."[9] But after September 1939 the young Ryga would not be alone and silent for long. That was the date when he entered Richmond Park school and began to learn English.

In later years Ryga recalled vividly an incident when he played truant from the school, and was severely disciplined for his sins. Yet despite his recollection of failing a grade, the young George Ryga was by the early 1940s Richmond Park's star pupil. Possibly even that early in his life he sensed that learning English would be a means of liberation from the narrow routines of the local Ukrainian farming families. In his "Essay on *A Letter to My Son*" Ryga would later write, harshly but accurately, of how functioning in a language other than Ukrainian led him to progressively disassociate himself from his ethnic community: "I turned away from survival by ethnicity at an early time in my life. My reasons were simple: I functioned in another language. And the cultural catch-basin of the small community was a convenient receptacle for social resentments, which, once voiced, became passive and ineffectual. And easily led to victimization by transplanted shepherds of the body and the soul. Marriages, careers, choices of places to live, all these were influenced not by enlarging awareness, but by commonly

23

shared limits to vision. I spoke the language, sang the songs, ate the food . . . but I could not, even as a boy, follow the ever-narrowing route of spiritual oblivion.''[10]

At some point in his early teens, George Ryga began to sense that there was a world beyond Richmond Park, and that education in the English language was the best, perhaps the only, path out of his community and into this wider world. Certainly he was motivated for success as a student. The Richmond Park school in those days taught up to grade eight. Ryga devoured those eight grades in seven years, completing his ''in school'' formal education in the summer of 1946, a month before his fourteenth birthday. That was too young to legally quit school, so the next fall he began taking courses from the Alberta Correspondence School. He was lucky to be assigned to an excellent English tutor, Nancy Thompson, who gave him the encouragement he needed to continue with his studies, but who also worked him hard and provided the critical comments he required to keep on improving. Under Nancy Thompson's wing he not only completed grade nine and decided to take senior high-school courses from the Correspondence School, he also began to write poetry. By 1947 he had written some verses of which he was sufficiently proud to submit them for publication to the local newspaper, the *Athabasca Echo*. The editor of the paper, Evelyn Rogers, encouraged him to keep writing, and also suggested works by well-known poets and other writers that he might like to read and perhaps use as models to learn from.

Together, then, Nancy Thompson and Evelyn Rogers put the Ukrainian teenager, who had learned English as a second language, in touch with the vast treasury of English literature that was waiting to be discovered. Ryga's principal means of discovery was the University of Alberta Extension Department's library service for rural communities. As he later recalled, ''For 30 cents I could get a hundred or two hundred books which were boxed and sent in, all I had to concern myself with was to get them back to the railway station, everything was prepaid . . . So most of the reading I ever did was done at that period of my life . . . It was hodge-podge: historical books, do-it-yourself manuals, fiction . . . This was my first contact with Shelley and Byron, and just learning that there was such a thing as history . . . Coming into contact with literature and becoming aware of its dignity, beauty, and severe discipline was probably the kind of challenge I needed at the time to begin to confront myself and to construct things on my own . . .''[11]

So in addition to working through the high-school courses, the young Ryga did a lot of intellectual exploring on his own, making mistakes and wasting some time, to be sure, but also finding the excitement and joy that comes with suddenly discovering authors that speak directly to one's own heart and mind. Working in this way and still lacking intellectual discipline, Ryga had a few conflicts with his distance-learning instructors. But they, and he, persevered up to grade eleven. Then the teenager faced a choice. It was not convenient for him to complete his high-school diploma entirely through correspondence because certain courses were not offered by the Correspondence School. He would have to move to Athabasca, enroll full time in the high school there, and live in lodgings while he studied. It was an option he seriously considered. But there was a problem, a financial one. How was he to pay for his room and board? His parents were barely surviving on the farm, they had no cash to spare. Moreover, now that he was legally old enough to work, going to school seemed a selfish luxury; the family could obviously use a wage-earner, especially as his father's health was now beginning to fail. Reluctantly the young man postponed further formal education and began instead to search for off-farm employment in the Athabasca area. He soon found that finding paid work was easier said than done. Jobs were not nonexistent, but they tended to be seasonal, episodic, and poorly paid. And, as Ryga later recalled, there was plenty of competition for the few work opportunities that existed: ''There was a bit of peripheral lumbering for two or three months in the year when civic projects came up, like repairing the road or building a bridge, so those of us who were of

employable age, which was fourteen and up, were vying for
these jobs with Indian lads from the reservation . . ."[12]

Ryga had previously met and made friends with native youths
who had worked on Richmond Park farms at harvest time, and
as something of an outsider in his local community he felt an
intuitive sympathy for these alien remnants of a formerly proud
and independent nation. His early poem "Indian Lament,"
revealed his understanding and respect for the culture and
heritage of the Indians and Métis who lived in the Calling Lake
region north-west of his parents' farm. It included the
following lines:

> My mother's song is the echo of northern rivers,
> My brothers are gone with the winds of autumn . . .
> Mighty were my people once — their footsteps now
> Are swept by the gales of time —
> Their cries have no voice . . .[13]

Now he met them as the dispossessed: poor and downtrod-
den wage-labourers trying to scratch a living on the margins
of white society; and discovered they were not so alien after
all. As he later explained the situation to Peter Hay, "We were
struggling exactly the same way to get out of the ghetto as
they were from the reserve . . . So there was that inter-
connection between the thoughts of the white community and
the thoughts of the Indian community. We were pretty much on
the same level; the only differences were cultural and
linguistic . . ."[14]

Ryga took whatever opportunities presented themselves to
talk to the native labourers and find out about their attitudes
to the white man's culture and to their own lives. He found
a sense of inferiority, resentment, and resignation: his Indian
acquaintances knew they were being given a raw deal, but
didn't know what to do about it, and were inclined to accept
their fate as a given and try to have a good time notwithstanding. They lived their lives fully, but recklessly — their
culture had lost its natural equilibrium. As Ryga later put it
in a newspaper interview about the factual background to his

play *Indian,* the Calling Lake natives "referred to themselves as 'breeds', for somehow they got the notion that mixed blood was superior . . . they were transient laborers, gay, naive, open hearted to the verge of being self-destructive. When they worked, their pace was fiendish. So were their excesses — fighting, drinking, gambling, and women. Yet they weren't oblivious to contradictions. I did some haying with a lad named Sammy. One of his arms was dead from disease and should have been amputated for it was obviously poisoning him. He would say: 'If God made all men same, then how come, misha, I so poor?' I never saw him after that summer."[15]

The Treaty Indians and Métis of the Athabasca area were no strangers to prejudice. They were regarded by most of the local inhabitants as the bottom of the social ladder, and they knew it. Ryga himself had not appreciated the pervasiveness of that kind of racial and ethnic prejudice until he came to visit Athabasca town frequently. As a child his first impression of Athabasca had been highly favourable; he remarks in "Notes on a Silent Boyhood" that when he "stared into the town of Athabasca for the first time" he thought to himself, "My God, what a beautiful city!"[16] Something of that naive wonder is captured in a series of scenes in "The Bridge" that portray the Athabasca known to Ryga as a youth — the local restaurant, a scene at the grain elevator, a wedding, sunsets flooding the river with orange light, and the atmosphere of the streets and waterfront at night one summer when the circus was in town. Here, for example, the boy Ryga is wandering at night among the railway tracks and lumber yards by the Athabasca River:

> He walked and drew deep breaths of the cool night
> air. The same river which flowed past the farm
> coursed its way through town. He walked to the
> muddy shore and looked into the water. It gurgled
> over some broken willow roots and invited him to
> jump on its ripples and ride home. He shook his head
> in protest and the river seemed to become harsher
> and louder, twisting faster and demanding he come

in. He walked away briskly toward the lumber yard with a vague thought of sleeping on one of the lumber piles. Turning into a narrow lane among the sweet-smelling drypiles of raw boards, he surprised a party of Indians drinking wine. They grabbed their wine jug and rose to flee, but seeing him, stopped and began laughing. "Have a drink," the fellow holding the jug pushed it under his face, "Good for you!" But he fled. The laughter of the dusky men followed him and was soon lost among the sharp lanes. He tried to walk out of the labyrinth, and began to panic when the piles appeared to spread far around him. They seemed to cover the town, and were closing in at the top to blot out the star-lit sky. He stumbled on at a run, turning corners this way and that. He fell across a naked couple making love. They were as frightened as he was, and he fled with no exchange of words. He found the street, and the lumber piles suddenly retreated back into the lumberyard . . . . The big doors of the hotel were open, and he strayed into the lobby. Here the air was warm and heavily scented with odors of cigar smoke and urine from the open doors of the lavatories. He sat down in a leather chair. A one-eyed old-age pensioner watched him from across the room and monotonously banged his pipe against a spit-riddled ashtray.[17]

Such segments from Ryga's first novel are very atmospheric; they are fragmentary images, to be sure, but powerful and vivid ones, evoking the lure of the town, its alien quality, and its dangers. So at first Athabasca seemed to Ryga strange and frightening, but also captivating. Later, as he came to know the town better, it became drearily familiar. But he also realised that the danger he had sensed as a child was real, that there was an underlying current of suppressed violence in this town, a violence that had roots in sexism and prejudice. Perhaps

Ryga's most successful attempt to capture in words the atmosphere of a small prairie town such as Athabasca (and especially the mood of violence lurking beneath the surface) was the previously unpublished fragment, "One October Evening." One can, in fact, recognise Athabasca here, thinly disguised. That fragment captures, too, the tense relationship between whites and natives, especially whites and native women, that Ryga found in the town. Furthermore, he learned that all whites were not regarded as equal there, and that he, as a working-class Ukrainian, was one of the inferior ones. It was a perception that reinforced his determination to master the English language and become a Canadian rather than an immigrant from eastern Europe. He later discussed this issue in an article in the *Canadian Theatre Review:*

> If you were born in the early thirties in what was predominantly a so-called ethnic community, you were quickly faced with a series of absolutes. Language absolutes which were to have a profound influence on your life and thoughts. The people around you, as well as small merchants in town — the poolhall operator, restaurant waitress, blacksmith, and grain elevator operator — spoke with the accent and phraseology you yourself used. But the ticket seller at the railway station, the social worker, the postmaster, and the old prick who fought in the First World War and now walked around town at night with a club in his hand in his capacity as town constable — all these spoke with an English accent. So when you heard an English accent, you heard state or civic authority or a lackey for the C.P.R. It was as clear-cut as that — there was "them" and there was "us."[18]

In his later teens, then, George Ryga developed a similar ambivalent relationship with Athabasca town, as he had had with the ethnic community of Richmond Park where he grew up. It would be wrong, however, to suggest that his overall attitude to Athabasca was hostile. The affection was there too. It comes out in the Athabasca verses he chose to include in *Song of My Hands*. "When the Sun Gets High," for example, gives a rollicking picture of the fun side of being a male teenager in Athabasca in the summers of the late '40s. It is more of a song than a poem, and Ryga in later years toyed with the idea of setting it to country and western music:

> When the sun gets high, I'm wonderin'
> What the old gang's doing now;
> It's been so long since we last met —
> So strong and sun-burnt brown,
> And walked the warm and dusty streets
> Of Athabasca town!
>
> We would load the cream and eggs
> On the back seat of the car
> And drive to sell them earliest
> Before the crowd came in,—
> And when the girls would leave to shop,
> We boys would gang around
> A table in the old pool hall
> In Athabasca town![19]

There were other poems, too, in *Song of My Hands* that captured something of the atmosphere of Athabasca on a weekend in the hot prairie summer. "The Country Fiddler," for example, alludes to the joyous occasion of a local fiddle contest at the annual County Fair, and "Maggie at the Union Dance" recalls the pleasures of dating and dancing at the downtown Parker's Hall. These unpretentious Athabasca lyrics only occasionally rise above the level of simple verse, yet they are valuable to us now as historical documents that pull from the air the vibrancy of life at a certain point in time and space. They are like old photographs, yet unlike photographs they evoke more than visual images. Ryga's early verse, though we must classify it as mainly juvenilia, still has the power to summon phantoms from the past.

Living and working in Athabasca was thus the first stage of George Ryga's life-journey away from Deep Creek and his ethnic origins. Since much of "The Bridge" is overtly autobiographical, it seems likely that the segment in the novel describing the young protagonist's experiences in a poultry-packing plant (and, subsequently, in a hospital) are based on Ryga's own memories of working in the town. The same is almost certainly true of his evocation of what it was like working for a winter in a logging camp, since seasonal employment in the forest industry is a significant element in the economy of the Athabasca region. But the opportunities for employment in Athabasca were — and remain — fairly limited, and when the young Ryga had the opportunity to leave for new pastures he accepted it enthusiastically. The last of this group of Athabasca poems, "Departure," an ingenuous yet poignant lyric, reflects the wrench of leaving home and venturing forth into the unknown. It ends with the stanzas:

> There is a road beyond the bridge,
> To lead you from your place of birth
> To farthest reaches of the earth . . .
> Away from field and forest ridge.

> You may return, or you may die —
> So wish them all a fond farewell,
> And hope that you may one day tell
> How man can live beneath this sky.[20]

The road beyond the bridge had led the young Ryga first to Athabasca. It would eventually lead him as far afield as Mexico and China. But first it wound its way, via Edmonton, to the Rocky Mountains.

BANFF AND EDMONTON, 1949-54

The opportunity that the young George Ryga found in 1949 to leave Richmond Park and Athabasca was not a job but a scholarship. Nancy Thompson had encouraged him to keep writing, not only the Burns-influenced romantic folk poetry that he was creating at this time, but also prose essays that required factual research and a disciplined compositional style. She had also brought to his attention a writing competition, sponsored by the Imperial Order of the Daughters of Empire and judged by the Alberta Writers Conference, for which the prize was a scholarship to the Banff School of Fine Arts Summer School on Creative Writing. Ryga submitted two essays, one on World War II (the manuscript of which is now unfortunately lost) and one on pioneer homesteading in Northern Alberta, "Smoke." He won the competition, "Smoke" was published in *The Correspondent* (a book celebrating the silver jubilee of the Correspondence School Branch of Alberta Education), and in the summer of 1949 George Ryga became a student at Banff. He later recalled in an interview for *The Ukrainian Canadian* that going to Banff was a milestone in his early life: "Banff turned out to be an interesting experience because it was the first time in my life I had been more than twenty miles from home. Banff was very good for me because I met Dr. E. P. Conklin from the University of Texas — one of the first great Americans that I'd met . . . Conklin was extremely good to me. It was he who first brought theatre to my attention. And Chekhov. I had never heard of Chekhov before . . ."[21]

At Banff, Ryga actually saw his first play, a student production of Sophocles' *Oedipus the King*, but at this time he was less interested in drama than in poetry and prose. He did well academically at Banff, and left the school with the realisation that it might just be possible to make a living as a writer rather than as a farmer or wage-labourer. The next year, 1950, one of his poems, "The Stray," appeared in print, in the *Athabasca Echo*, and he won a second IODE scholarship to Banff. For this summer school his teachers included Jerome Lawrence, an American playwright and commercial writer of some renown. Lawrence quickly recognised Ryga as the most talented of that summer's bunch of aspiring authors, and set out to train him intensively in the mechanics of the trade. Ryga responded to the special attention, and worked hard to justify the confidence placed in him. Looking back on that important summer, he commented to Peter Hay that "of all the catalysts working for me, Jerry was probably the most significant. He worked me very very hard. In fact I stayed with him in his cottage and the workday began at seven in the morning and didn't end till midnight every night. I had to keep the same pace he did, and it was brutal: the criticism, the pressures that were put on . . . Because he knew — he began to put together the elements of my background — and he knew that unless he punched in everything he could within those six weeks I'd probably vanish and wouldn't surface again . . . Three or four years ago I visited him in Los Angeles and he said to me: 'I didn't honestly think you'd make it, frankly, because all the elements were stacked against you . . .'"[22]

The young Ryga again performed very well at Banff, but one incident that occurred that summer resulted in his being debarred from any future IODE scholarships. He wrote an anti-war poem, deploring the Korean War, for a student magazine, and copies of the poem, distributed on the streets of Banff, reached the hands of his sponsors. They were not amused, and made their views known to the young student-writer in no uncertain terms. It was the first of several occasions on which George Ryga was to be blacklisted for his political opinions and for his forthrightness in expressing them.

No more scholarships to Banff meant that Ryga was soon back in Athabasca looking for a job, any job. He found one next winter working in a construction gang, building a bridge over the Athabasca River, just north of the town of Athabasca. It was hard, gruelling, and dangerous work, but the youth found in his gang leader, Dave Stirling, a true friend who taught him much about politics and literature as well as some rudiments of mechanical engineering. Stirling was a militant unionist and socialist of Scottish extraction who read Marxist theory and loved Romantic poetry. Ryga recalled in "Notes from a Silent

Boyhood" that Stirling introduced him to the poetry of Byron and to left-wing "books and newspapers that explained and took sides on great issues of the day," from which he obtained an ideological framework he had previously lacked. From then on, Ryga added, "all the parts began falling into place." He now knew that he not only wanted to be a writer, he wanted to be a socially aware, politically committed writer. He also knew he had a great deal of reading to do, in the realms of philosophy and politics, as well as world literature.[23]

One day in the early winter months of 1951, Ryga's job helping construct the Athabasca bridge came to an abrupt end. His right hand was caught in a pulley, and in a few tragic seconds two fingers and part of a third were torn off. Ryga never wrote a detailed account of how this industrial accident happened, but in *Beyond the Crimson Morning* he did recall a similar incident that he had witnessed while working on a local farm:

> On the farms that autumn were youth from Ontario who had come west. Youth from mining communities and youth from the cities. One such was Roger, who hired on to the crew on which I worked. He was a handsome, muscular apprentice in carpentry who had taken a few weeks to see the countryside beyond his native Guelph. He was an athlete who ran and whooshed his breath by moonlight. He did calisthenics each morning in the barnyard, the surprised chickens clucking around him and blinking in the early sunlight while the rest of us serviced equipment, sang ditties, and complained of imaginary abuses.
>
> "Stan's wife fed us roasted dog last night. He was clawin' at my guts all night . . ."
>
> "Johnnie Fedoruk of Istwith liked to play with the thing that he pissed with . . ."
>
> And then the sound of a door slamming, and the enormous belly of old Ignace, the farmer, preceding him to the porch. "Awright, awright — enough! You

boys got no respect. No respect at all. The missus is inside — she can hear them dirty songs. Shame on you, boys.''

His eyes moved across the barnyard. He saw Roger lifting his prone body up and down, sweat glistening on his brown back and sinewy arms. The old man's face glowed in admiration.

"That boy sure got a lot of vinegar left to be doing them push-ups. Me? I hardly got enough poop left to raise this cup of tea to my mouth this early in the morning.'' Then he relieved himself of a large burp and waddled down the steps for an inspection of our work. In half an hour the equipment would be worked to capacity. As would we.

That afternoon Roger and I were called off the fields to man the truck that brought wheat from the threshing units to the storage granaries. The truck was loaded from a grain hopper off the threshing machine. We would then drive half a mile to the storage buildings and unload it with a portable auger, which was mounted on the grain box of the truck. Roger hated grain dust. So I shoveled the wheat around the storage building while he operated the auger outside.

Over the roar and throb of equipment I hear him singing, "Oh, the ring-dang-do, oh, what is that? So big and fat, like a pussy cat . . . '' Then he screamed with a long, plaintive outcry that made me freeze in mid-action, a loaded grain scoop raised in my hands. The auger churned away. A moment later Roger's hand, severed at the wrist, fell with the wheat pouring from the end of the auger spout . . . .[24]

Ryga's own accident landed him in the Athabasca hospital for a few days, an experience he drew upon when writing "The Bridge.'' His slow convalescence gave him plenty of time for reflection, and he came to realise that, notwithstanding all its pain and inconvenience, his injury might prove useful in one way. Partially handicapped as he now was, he was less useful as a manual labourer or farm worker. That meant there would be less opposition from his father and mother to his taking a white-collar job. In short, the industrial accident gave him the excuse for which he had been looking to not take over the family farm. Ryga now renewed his search for a writing job, and, armed with the prestige of the IODE scholarships and a letter of recommendation from Jerome Lawrence, he eventually found one. It consisted of script writing for an Edmonton radio station, CFRN. He now moved to Edmonton, shared an apartment with a fellow CFRN worker, Jerry Sykes, and held down his first (and, as it turned out, only) job as a member of the Canadian intellectual proletariat for about three years.

Those first Edmonton years were important ones in Ryga's intellectual and political growth. He was still eager to learn, despite his failure to earn a high-school diploma and the slightly sour end to his student days at the Banff School of Fine Arts, so he began auditing evening courses run by the University of Alberta Department of Extension. Over the next few years he sat in on quite a few, ranging from music and Russian to philosophy and English literature. Before long he was part of a circle of left-wing students who spent much of their spare time arguing about philosophy and art and the remainder doing grass-roots leg work for the Cooperative Commonwealth Federation or the Canadian Communist Party. Sometime between 1952 and 1954 Ryga became an avid reader of the socialist literary periodical *New Frontiers*, joined the Canadian Communist Party, and also became an ardent supporter of the Canadian Peace Council. He was soon supplementing his reading of the Romantic poets with classics by such founding fathers of the radical democratic and socialist tradition as Tom Paine and Karl Marx, and with the works of Pablo Neruda, Lorca, and Jean-Paul Sartre. During this period he continued writing poetry, and one of his best efforts, "Federico García Lorca," was in fact published in *New Frontiers* in 1954.[25]

On the surface it looked as though Ryga had now broken

free of the family farm, Richmond Park, and Athabasca. He could, it seemed, look forward to a career in radio and perhaps, eventually, TV as an in-house script-writer and producer. But the call of family and farm, though weakened and distant, could still be felt and heard. Occasionally it became too loud and strong to resist, as Ryga recalled in *Beyond the Crimson Morning*:

Twenty five years ago one autumn in northern Alberta. A bumper grain crop and a shortage of farm labor to harvest it. I was a junior employee at a commercial radio station in the city, a first-generation wage earner in a family whose long history in Europe did not evolve beyond neo-feudalism. The seasons of each year in my early life were the times of seeding, growth, and harvests.

A telephoned message left on my desk said: "Heavy frost last night. We need help." That evening I was riding back to the community of my birth on an unpaid, unscheduled holiday which my co-workers in the city neither understood nor sanctioned. "What a peculiar thing to do — go out and help farmers take crops in. Farmers never come to the city to help merchants."

It had been in the midst of an aimless, sad discussion of reason chiding instinct which replayed in my mind that evening as the express bus going north bumped and swayed over the gravel highways of my early years into the soft blue northern night. I attempted no explanation of my sudden departure from the city. It was an instinctual response coming from deep within me. Knowing I had no explanation that would not sound ridiculous, I was ashamed of my helplessness. All I knew was that there was no work or consideration more important than the harvesting of food. Death, illness, personal disaster — all these had to be set aside when the landsman raced approaching winter for possession of precious kernels of grain or bundles of vegetables.[26]

The young radio producer and budding writer was still a farm-boy at heart. But he was also now a rank-and-file Communist militant, and what Ryga found increasingly difficult during the early mid-1950s, in the climate of the Cold War, was keeping his radical political beliefs separate from his work as a script-writer at CFRN. Much of his writing for the radio station was hack work, but he was clearly capable of better, and the station manager soon recognised this and gave him the task of scrip-ting and producing his own program. It was a literary hour spon-sored by the Edmonton Druggists Association, called "Reverie." Ryga successfully carried out this assignment for several years, but in November 1953 he went (at least in the station manager's eyes) too far. He produced a special Armis-tice Day edition of "Reverie" which presented the writings of various pacifist First World War poets interspersed with anti-war music. Ryga remembers the incident as follows:

" . . . then I got a job writing and producing a radio program in Edmonton. I stayed there about three years, and finally lost the job over a memorable Remembrance Day program that we produced. We took some of the works of Pablo Neruda, William Carlos Williams and Robert Service, and we used one line from 'Flanders Fields', then a poem by Williams, and then 'In Flanders Fields the poppies blow,' followed by another poem, then 'between the crosses row on row.' This was all carefully researched, including the tremendous amount of anti-war music that was beginning to bloom at the time. So that was the last show I did. When that show was aired it was Remembrance Day and this was so totally different from the usual Remembrance Day programming that the show was cancelled right off. But the curious thing was that about six months later the predecessors of the Board of Broadcast Governors were visiting radio stations in western Canada to see what type of original material they were turning out, and this was the show which was played for these gentlemen, as an example of the creativity of Edmonton radio. So they got their plaudits out of it, even though I lost the show . . ."[27]

The program caused a storm of controversy. Listeners' reactions were mixed: CFRN received calls and letters praising it as well as hysterical and angry ones denouncing Ryga as a "conchie" and a "red." The Druggist Association, a little surprisingly, defended Ryga's artistic integrity, and this probably saved him from instant dismissal by CFRN. From then on, however, his writing was suspect, and he was on probation. The next year the axe fell. Asked to give a speech at a local pro-Rosenberg rally, he took the risk of exercising his democratic right to freedom of speech, and paid the penalty. Fired from CFRN, he joined the unemployed on the streets of Edmonton. It was not an enviable experience, but he used his new-found time to write more poetry and to jot down on paper scenes remembered from his childhood. The poems would soon find their way into *Song of My Hands*, and the prose fragments would eventually be used in his first novel, "The Bridge." If "The Bridge" can be taken as strict autobiography, Ryga did eventually find work compiling an Edmonton street directory, but this city employment was shortlived, and in the winter of 1954-55 he headed north again. The lure was a tough but lucrative season of work in a logging camp, another experience recorded in "The Bridge." Ryga endured it because he needed the money for two new projects: to finance the publication of his collection of poems, *Song of My Hands*, and to help pay for a new adventure, an extended trip to Europe. He decided to give Europe first priority.

EUROPE, 1955-56

George Ryga's European adventure began in the spring of
1955. With the money he had saved from his years at CFRN
and his stint as a lumberjack he bought a boat ticket to England
and hitchhiked to Montreal to catch the Cunard liner. His
journey east is recorded in three forms: in the manuscript
novel, "The Bridge," in two poems included in *Song of My
Hands*, "Summer Journey" and "Lines written in Northern
Ontario," and in an epic poem he wrote in 1959, *These Songs
I Sing*. To judge from these manuscripts, Ryga greatly enjoyed
the anarchic freedom of hitchhiking and that mentally exhilarating
sense of the vastness of Canada that comes only from traversing
on the ground the unending expanse of prairie and forest between Alberta and Eastern Ontario. His joy at embarking on
this great adventure is reflected in the following lines from *These
Songs I Sing*:

> I slept the sleep of forgotten men
> Deep in Algonquin country, —
> Dreaming the dreams of the hungry,
> For I have always been terribly poor
> And my passport to life
> Was a sheaf of verse in my hip pocket;
> I dreamed the dreams of the road —
> "Un Canadien errant . . ."
> Was the song of the heaving waters
> Of the Great Lakes
> Early in the day —
> Commerce passed me on the road
> In late-model cars
> But the sun was in my face
> And in my blood —
> Lazy seagulls paged me
> In the blue, blue sky
> And I was completely,
> Unbelievably, happy.[28]

On the way east Ryga spent a few days in Toronto with some literary friends whose love of folk music reinforced his desire to find out what was happening in folk circles in England. When he arrived in London he found the first phase of the English Folk Revival in full swing. Scottish singer, musicologist and writer Ewan MacColl was the leading promoter of indigenous British folk music in the mid-1950s, and had organised the first London folk club, at the Princess Louise pub in High Holborn. By the time Ryga arrived in London, MacColl had recruited helpers from among such doyens of Anglo-Celtic folk music as Bert Lloyd and Seamus Ennis, and had also involved in his project visiting American ethnomusicologist Alan Lomax and the man who was to become known as the father of British blues, Alexis Korner. These talented enthusiasts put together a program called "Blues and Ballads," which they staged at the Princess Louise and other London venues[29]. It proved an excellent means for Ryga to learn rapidly about the Celtic and English folk traditions, and he was fortunate to meet not only Lomax, one of the most renowned experts on North American folk music and folk culture, but also MacColl, a great authority on Scottish balladry and himself a folk-poet of industrial Britain. Ryga's own interest in folk music as poetry was to be reflected in some of the lyrics in *Song of My Hands*, in the epic *These Songs I Sing*, and in the use of folk song in *The Ecstasy of Rita Joe*.[30]

Ryga's first stay in London was brief. He had a mission to accomplish, representing the Alberta branch of the Canadian Peace Council at a Congress of World Peace in Helsinki, Finland. He hoped to see some of his political and cultural heroes (Bertrand Russell, Jean-Paul Sartre, Pablo Neruda, and Ilya Ehrenburg, among others) in action at close quarters, and to participate, if only in a small way, in the struggle to end the Cold War and to prevent World War III. At Helsinki he met and became close friends with three people who influenced him considerably: the American poet Martha Millet, the Turkish writer Nazim Hikmet, and a New Zealand author who had made China his home, Rewi Alley.[31] It was Alley, above all, who made

Ryga aware of the problems of the Third World, of the work of various United Nations economic and cultural organisations, and of the successes and difficulties of the Chinese Revolution. Ryga wrote about Alley in the *Athabasca Echo* in 1956, describing him in the following terms:

> I met Rewi Alley in Helsinki, where we both served on the Cultural Commission working on recommendations for exchanges of cultures, to be submitted to the United Nations . . . . Many and wonderful were the stories he told me, of his boyhood in New Zealand, the months as a young man when he laboured on an Australian farm, the many years of the sea when he travelled the length and breadth of the world. Then the eventful years when he went to China to teach school, and worked for the co-operatives in that vast country, finally turning to a life of letters, and blossoming into one of the most prolific poets and authors of his time. So China became the homeland of this powerfully built, lonely man. And he gave much for China. He not only took part in rebuilding the country and teaching her people, he also took part in the heroic march of the Eighth Army, when they grew from a handful of soldiers into one of the greatest armies in the world, to sweep from Chinese soil the Japanese invaders. Today Rewi Alley is back in China, walking up and down the country as he has done for almost forty years . . . an admired artist with millions of friends about him.[32]

Here was a man who had successfully combined a literary career with real, effective, practical, political and education work. He had helped improve the lives of millions, and he was a true "people's artist." In short, he was just what Ryga himself longed to be. Ryga left Helsinki in culture shock, bemused but elated. He now had a global vision, and in men such as Sartre, Neruda, and Alley he had role models of what a socialist writer should be. His project from now on would be to try to work out what a Western Canadian version of a similarly "committed" or *engagé* writer would be like. But first he still had some travel plans. One of these was visiting Poland. He didn't get as far as the south-western Ukraine, which was now part of the Soviet Union, but he did get to Warsaw, and, as a result of connections he had made in Helsinki, was invited to do a broadcast for Radio Poland on another of his favourite poets, Walt Whitman. This bit of work helped his finances considerably, and allowed him to travel further in Eastern Europe and to attend a World Youth Festival in Bulgaria.

Ryga's experiences in Poland and Bulgaria, like his visit to Finland, had a significant impact on his political outlook. They made him aware of the bureaucratic and statist character of East European communism. But they also developed his ideas on the role of literature in society. He began to have a better understanding of the powerful role that literature can play in developing the consciousness of the masses in Third World countries. Writers, he realised, could be useful agents in the revolutionary struggle against political and cultural imperialism. As he recalled in conversation with Peter Hay, "There were people from Ghana with a very no-nonsense attitude to literature, to art, to folk forms like the dance. They were reinterpreting everything and it was like watching a laboratory. It was all part of a larger process . . . Years later this influenced me in many judgements I had to make about my own country, when we caught up with our own anti-colonial struggle, because that's what we are in today, at least in the early stages of it . . ."[33]

Another very important thing that happened to Ryga in Bulgaria was a brief but intense love affair with a Persian poet, Lobat Valat. He described this relationship in *Beyond the Crimson Morning*:

> Twenty-three years ago. We met in Bulgaria in a camp for holidaying cultural workers outside of Plovdiv. In the month of August, when the plums and tobacco were being harvested in the fertile valleys. Her tenderness and enthusiasm for life took us down dusty roads into villages as ancient as Macedonia

itself. Her curiosity, and the curiosity she excited in me took us into crumbling peasant homes with chickens in the courtyard, surrounded by grapevines that drooped low to the earth under their load of golden fruit, sweet and aromatic as honey. And in the shade of the vines and jasmine, old men drowsing, their white moustaches draping over their chins, their eyes clear and fierce as they recalled old and recent battles in the long, turbulent history of their homeland. One such old man waved to us with a hand as gnarled as the branch of a desert oak tree.

"Come inside, young people. We will have wine and some words together. The world does not arrive at my doorstep every afternoon."

Our arms about each other, we sat on his bench and drank his wine and listened to his long, ferocious tales of life, of love, and of the ironies of the gods when they interceded in the fortunes of the family, the fields, or the state . . . .

That night at the cave of Orpheus with a melancholy moon illuminating luxuriant forests in its baleful light she had the first of her excruciating encounters with pain. Her face knotted, she screamed words and denials in the language of her ancestors. I bathed her and held her in my lap, speaking assurances that were desperate, hollow, and meaningless as she trembled and talked quickly of resistance to the medievalists in Teheran. Of imprisonment and torture, and the assaults on her heart and nervous system. The electrode scars on her cheek glowed as if activated again by the machinery of torture. Her luminous eyes filled with tears, trickling down her face and drying into white dust by morning. She knew she was dying. She had been released and permitted to leave her homeland to die. And despite her resolve she was now afraid, for she was young and a mother.

"I had two children. Nobody will tell me where

they were taken. I will never see my children
again . . ."[34]

Ryga's passionate involvement with Lobat Valat, brought
home to him in a personal way the horrors of living under any
military and authoritarian regime. For the moment he remained
a communist — at least nominally — but his first-hand experience
of communist bureaucracy in Eastern Europe had made him
think twice about so readily equating Stalinist communism with
the socialist ideals he had espoused for the last five years. The
determination of the intellectual leaders of the peace movement,
Sartre and Russell, to steer a neutral course between the two
Super Powers, had impressed him deeply. He remained committed to the twin causes of world peace and social revolution, but
he had growing doubts about where the USSR stood in relation
to these goals. His hopes for the future were passing from
Russia to the nonaligned nations and the Third World.

Ryga's travels in Europe thus brought him a degree of disenchantment as well as opening new horizons for him. He returned
to England less naive, more experienced in the ways of the
world and in the ways of love, but also emotionally shattered.
Lobat and he were reluctant to part, but there was no future
in their relationship. She eventually went back to Eastern Europe
in the hope of resuming her literary and revolutionary activity
there. Ryga treasured her memory, and wrote a passionate
poem about her on the theme of resurrection and renewed
struggle, entitled "My Song Is Still." He would include it in
his first publication, *Song of My Hands*. These are the opening two stanzas of the poem:

> I cannot see the sun,
> Nor hear the music of the summer
> When scented mists
> Diffuse the distant hills.
>
> For death, whose icy claws
> I have beaten from my breast
> Now shades with ashen grey
> Your gentle, lovely face.[35]

Back in Britain, Ryga looked for and found a job working for the BBC. It wasn't the kind of script writing and radio production that he really wanted, but it was easy and enjoyable: watching and listening to BBC productions and writing reviews of them for use by daily newspapers and magazines. During these months, early in 1956, he met for the first time his future wife, Norma Campbell. Ryga enjoyed living in London, and although he had a return boat ticket to Canada in his wallet he at one point even considered making England his home. But the Russian invasion of Hungary completed his disenchantment with Stalinist communism, and that made social relations more difficult with such London Communists as MacColl with whom he had previously been on good terms. Then the Suez crisis brought home to him the realisation that if he became a British citizen he might be liable for active military service. Two friends, the violinists Sergei Bezkorvany and his wife, had suddenly vanished from the London music scene after Sergei, who held joint British and Canadian citizenship, had been served with draft papers. George finally found Sergei working as a janitor in an Underground station, and together they decided they had seen enough of Europe for the time being. Ryga cashed in his Cunard ticket and bought passage for the three of them on a mail packet to Halifax. It was a long, rough voyage, and they arrived back in Canada seasick and penniless. Although winter had now set in, Ryga had no alternative but to hitchhike back to Alberta, a journey far less pleasant than his eastward idyll in the spring of 1955.[36] But he eventually made it back to the family farm. Athabasca was not so easily abandoned as he had imagined when he set out eighteen months before.

EDMONTON, 1956-61

On returning to Edmonton, Ryga looked for a job in radio, expecting that his experience with CFRN, Radio Poland, and the BBC would stand him in good stead. He found all doors closed to him, except for some occasional free-lance work. In despair he took a job with a local advertising agency, but found the work distasteful, and after a while decided that he would prefer manual labour to this kind of commercial writing. So for close on two years, manual labour it was: as a carpenter, cook, waiter, dry cleaner, furniture remover, and, naturally enough, farm-hand. The farm work was mainly on his parents' farm; George still steadfastly refused to take over the farm from his father, but he was always ready to help with the ploughing or the harvest. Earning his living in this "catch as catch can" fashion, the young author sometimes found that weeks or months would pass by without his setting pen to paper. But he had not given up his ambition to become a professional writer, and when inspiration moved him he added to his stock of unpublished manuscripts. He was also determined that they should not all remain unpublished, and in late 1956 he gathered together many of the poems he had written during the previous few years and published them himself as *Song of My Hands*. From a financial perspective the project was moderately successful since the limited edition sold out rapidly and Ryga recouped his capital investment. The venture did not do much to further his literary career, however, because Ryga lacked the means to publicize the work and it attracted little critical attention.[37]

The readers of this slim volume found an uneven collection of verse. Some may, in retrospect, be dismissed as juvenilia: all too obvious imitations of the English Romantics and Robert Burns or attempts at folk poetry that only occasionally rise above commonplace verse. But amidst the dross and the first drafts could be found some gems: the simple, but beautifully crafted pastoral lyrics "Twilight" and "Summer Rain," for example, or the stark images of "Scenes That Come and Go," in which the poet recalls "a stony face in a stony field, the wind-torn cloud in the autumn sky." Some of Ryga's early poetry that may not win plaudits from literary critics is nonetheless valuable for what it reveals about its author's perspective on farming in Northern Alberta and on life as a teenager in Athabasca. Three poems in *Song of My Hands*, "Song of the Farmer," "The Neighbouring Farmer" and "My Land" express the young Ryga's respect and sympathy for the pioneer homesteader and, in particular, his forceful recognition of the back-breaking toil required to make a success of working a small farm on the kind of marginal land found in the Richmond Park region. "My Land" is particularly interesting for its ideological message; here the young Ryga combines his love of nature, his defence of the farmer, his respect for the ordinary Canadian working man, his national pride, and his socialist hostility to bankers and capitalists in a poem that is still, in essence, a pastoral elegy. Another lyric, "Prairie Wind," develops the theme of "My Land" by spanning and drawing together the two sides of the province of Alberta: the rural farmlands and the industrial towns. It demonstrates the young poet's love of Alberta and his fundamental optimism about its future:

> Traveller, when you see my country
> Where prairie wind and sun range free;
> Remember those who found and built her —
> Think of what she yet will be![38]

In a few of the poems Ryga aimed higher. In "My Song Is Still," "As Men Have Seen Him," "Our Songs Are those of May Birds," and "Federico García Lorca" he created more complex, multi-faceted images with harder, deeper, and more resonant messages. This poetry was still political in ambiance, but beyond question it was also carefully crafted and highly effective literature. As an example we may quote "Federico García Lorca" in its entirety.

FEDERICO GARCÍA LORCA

Spanish patriot and poet — shot by a fascist firing squad in Granada, 1936

> With fire in his wild eyes
> He turned to go . . . then paused,

And defiantly replied the taunting chant
" . . . you're mad . . . you're mad!"

"Mad! Yes, mad as the flowers
In the sunlit field;—
Or the stars in our Spanish night,
Who weep with me at what has come to pass . . .
If I am mad,
Then mad is our sobbing earth
That whispers, "Free me,
So I may dream with you,
My glorious children!"
Mad? Then so were the souls
Of our fathers,
Whose lovely books you burned
In the village court.
Mad as my poems,
Whose verse froze upon your lips
In fear,
When they hushed with sword and flame
The songs of free men.
I go, but let my madness live
In the hungry hills,
And not in the sunless dungeon."

Proudly, he walked the dusty road;—
And through the silent, shamed mob,
Passed a sob, as of a frightened child . . .[39]

The late 1950s became a time of restless uncertainty in
Ryga's life. He toyed with the idea of taking a B.A. through
the University of Alberta Department of Extension, but he was
reluctant to give up the freedom to follow his own political and
intellectual interests wheresoever they led him. One, his love
of Robbie Burns, led him to Scotland. For several years now
Ryga had been a fervent admirer of the poetry of Burns whom
he saw as a fellow poverty-stricken son of the soil trying to
articulate the ideas and values of a rural minority culture. Scottish folklorist Ewan MacColl, whom Ryga had met in London

49

in 1955-56, shared his enthusiasm, and had showed him how Burns' poetry was deeply rooted in Scottish folklore and folk song. This insight had reinforced Ryga's desire to study Burns in greater depth and to see for himself the countryside that Burns had written about. By 1959 he had saved enough money to take a second working vacation in Europe. To carry out his program of sightseeing and research, Ryga rented a bicycle and cycled around Scotland, going as far north as the Isle of Skye but then returning south to Dumfries and the border country beloved of Burns. In Dumfries he set to work on his research project, visiting Burns scholar James Barke and examining Burns' original manuscripts in the local archives.[40] His close examination of the roots of Burns' creativity reinforced Ryga's own determination to write folk poetry — that is, poetry using the language of the common folk and dealing with their own lives, perceptions and emotions. As Ryga later remarked in an interview, ''I went to Scotland and researched Robert Burns and folklore, studying the effects of folklore upon writing. Burns, of course, was a beautiful study because he was one of the closest to the soil and conditions of life in his times . . .''[41] Ryga subsequently explained to Peter Hay that at that time "there were two writers in my mind who had special significance. One of them was Burns, the other the Ukrainian poet, Shevchenko. Both of them did the same thing with language: they elevated it, they took it from a very colloquial form into a new art form . . .''[42]

Studying Burns in depth seems to have rekindled Ryga's determination to be a politically committed creative writer. He recalled this period of his life in an interview with Jerry Shack in 1969. It was, he remembered, a time during which he drifted for several years but then gradually settled down to complete his apprenticeship to the craft of writing:

> ''Well, when I returned to Canada, to a job that was non-existent, I did something quite different. I went back to basic manual work: working in a hotel, worked at carpentry, did some stints back on the farm where

my folks were still living — and I wrote poetry in my spare time. Back in 1956 I published my first collection of poetry (forty or so poems) and it sold out within a month. At this time writing was quite easy for me because weeks or even months could go by before I'd write a poem, since I was doing something else . . . About 1958 or '59 I started to return to writing in a much more disciplined, organized way. I began to tackle the problems of style and content, craft, trying to utilize all the sort of free-forming things that were happening to me into a concise and usable form. This was when I started writing short stories. At the time, the only market for that type of thing was CBC. Most of my stuff ended up in Winnipeg for regional broadcast . . ."[43]

Three other things helped him return to serious writing. He was reading voraciously, and came across other authors with whom he felt a special kinship of the spirit. In particular, he devoured the complete works of Dostoevsky, and found in these writings and those of other Russian novelists the inspiration to write his own tales about his rural homeland. Three works served as models: Gogol's *Dead Souls*, Dostoevsky's *Poor Folk*, and Sholokov's *Tales from the Don*. A second blessing was finding a routine job that kept body and soul together but did not tax him mentally or physically, thereby leaving him time and energy for creative work. Working as a night-clerk at the Selkirk Hotel in Edmonton allowed for many hours of solitary reading and scribbling when guests were asleep and all was quiet at the front desk. Ryga kept a sort of diary of the bizarre incidents that sometimes occurred at the hotel, and drew on this material when he wrote his third published novel, *Night Desk* (1976).[44]

The other important leap forward for Ryga in the late 1950s was the resumption of his relationship with Norma Campbell. Norma, a Nova Scotian by birth, returned to Canada in the summer of 1958, and then a year later moved to Edmonton to live with her sister, an acquaintance of George's. When George returned from Scotland in August the two quickly became friends again, and by the end of the year had decided to set up house together. Norma had two daughters by a previous marriage, and the Rygas soon added to their family, with Campbell born in 1961 and Sergei in 1963. Norma worked full time as a medical photographer at the University of Alberta, George quit the Selkirk Hotel to become a house-husband, and he also held down a part-time job at the Post Office, mainly doing sorting, which afforded him flexible hours, plus a fairly decent wage. In his spare time, such as it was, he got down to some serious writing. From 1960 onwards a stream of manuscripts flowed from his typewriter, each bearing the return address 10603-81 St., Edmonton, where he and Norma lived until 1963.[45]

George Ryga's primary ambition at this time had become writing a successful novel. He had plenty of ideas, and now resolved to take the time needed to work them out in detail. The results of some twenty months' labour, crouched day after day at the typewriter, were the first drafts of six full-length novels, plus at least eight short stories. The novels were titled "The Bridge," "Night Desk," "The Hungry Hills," "Old Sam," "Wagoner Lad," and "Thy Sawdust Temples." Of these, the manuscripts of three ("Old Sam," "Thy Sawdust Temples," and "Wagoner Lad") have apparently been lost. "The Bridge," which was heavily autobiographical in spirit and often in detail as well, was a *bildungsroman* that describes the childhood and adolescence of a farm-boy from Alberta who leaves home to find work in the city and then travels east to Toronto, Montreal, England, Scotland, and Poland. "Night Desk" went through several metamorphoses, including a temporary name change to "Last of the Gladiators," before it eventually found a publisher over a decade later, and in fact the final text bears very little resemblance to the first draft, although the setting and ambiance of the novel are the same. "The Hungry Hills" was thus the only one of the six with which Ryga had fairly immediate success; the second draft was published by Longmans in 1963 as *Hungry Hills* (a slightly revised version was also published by Talonbooks in 1974).[46]

Initially, however, Ryga received rejection slips for all six novels, and it was probably only the support and encouragement he received from Norma that kept his ambition to be a novelist alive through repeated disappointments. Happily, too, he found that there was more of a market for short stories. The market was CBC Winnipeg, which found occasional airtime to broadcast "High Noon and Long Shadows," "Gold in the Aspens," "The Wife of Sid Malan" (all written in 1960), "Betrothal," and "A Touch of Cruelty" (written in 1961). Ryga also wrote some other short stories in these years: "The Meek Shall Inherit," "Golden Boy," "Glow Worm on the Beach," and "Business Man's Dilemma," but only the manuscript of the first of these seems to have been preserved. The relative receptiveness of CBC Winnipeg to his stories reminded Ryga of his experience as a radio script-writer and producer, and now, for the first time, he began thinking seriously about writing plays. He first dramatised two of his best short stories, "Gold in the Aspens" and "A Touch of Cruelty," and then he tried his hand at creating a drama from scratch. The result was "Village Crossroad," an interesting and powerful piece that deserves to be rescued from obscurity. But it was the dramatised version of another short story, "The Pinetree Ghetto," that would make Ryga's mark as a professional dramatist.[47]

BREAKTHROUGH, 1962

Nineteen Sixty-two was the year of breakthrough for George Ryga, the year that he first achieved cross-Canada recognition as an author. The burst of creativity that had sustained him through small victories and huge, disheartening setbacks during the first two years of the new decade continued in the third. In 1962 he wrote the first draft of a new novel, initially called "Recollections of a Stone-Picker," later renamed "A Forever Kid," and eventually published in London in 1966 by Michael Joseph as *Ballad of a Stone-Picker*.[48] Ryga now felt more confident of his vocation as a writer, and he believed that "Stone-Picker," notwithstanding the initial rejection slips, was the best novel he had yet created. He continued writing short stories inspired by the landscape and inhabitants of Richmond Park and Athabasca. Six new ones, three of which were purchased by the CBC, flowed from his pen that year: "Nellie-Boy," "Brothers," "Love by Parcel Post," "Legacy of the Meek," "Half-Caste," and "The Pinetree Ghetto." Two of these, "Legacy" and "Ghetto," used fiction as a vehicle for studying the fate of disadvantaged social groups and therefore had a more overtly political edge than the other Athabasca stories. The harder hitting of the two, "The Pinetree Ghetto," Ryga considered his most powerful short story to date, and was surprised and dismayed to find it rejected as too political by CBC Winnipeg. He decided to rework it for another medium, television. In *The Ukrainian Canadian* he explained to Jerry Shack how he came to have a big hit with the TV play "Indian":

> "I wasn't getting anyplace. The 10, 15 or 20 dollars I'd get paid for a story hardly paid for the paper used. And then we got our first television set . . . and I noticed a program called 'Quest' on CBC, produced out of Toronto. I had done a short story called 'The Pinetree Ghetto' and sent it to Winnipeg, and the man from CBC who had so far been buying everything I sent in, returned 'The Pinetree Ghetto.' His criticism was 'you are allowing your social convictions to interfere with your ability as a writer, and you're going downhill, boy.' But I liked the story very much and I thought: 'screw him . . .' I sent it in directly to 'Quest.' That play kicked around on the desks of script readers in Toronto for two or three months until Daryl Duke was going through scripts

one day and pulled this thing out . . . He read it, and he wired me, and within three or four days he was casting. But before they started shooting they came out to Edmonton to check conditions and see if the situation described in the play was for real, you know? Well they spent two days and became convinced it was. Well, this was my big breakthrough because when it was aired it had a fantastic reaction. Right across the country. *Maclean's* magazine picked it up and published it and suddenly I found new possibilities open to me."[49]

The success of "Indian" opened doors for Ryga as a television dramatist, and much of his output during the remainder of the decade was written for this medium. He undoubtedly learned his craft as a playwright through writing for television, an experience that had a significant impact on his style as a stage dramatist and in part explains the cinematographic character of such plays as *The Ecstasy of Rita Joe* or *Sunrise on Sarah*.[50] But Ryga also learned in 1962-3 that success as a television writer doesn't necessarily mean that publishers will welcome your novels and short stories. In the wake of *Maclean's* feature on "Indian" he packaged the play together with the ten short stories he considered his best ("Gold in the Aspens," "Legacy of the Meek," "Betrothal," "High Noon and Long Shadows," "Love by Parcel Post," "Half-Caste," "The Wife of Sid Malan," "Nellie-Boy," "A Touch of Cruelty," and "Brothers") as "Poor People," a title chosen in the hope that its allusion to Dostoevsky's early work with a similar name would clue potential publishers and their readers into what its author was aiming to achieve in the book.[51]

The strategy did not work. More rejection slips piled up on the Ryga desk. Frustrated in his attempt to publish a collection of Athabasca tales, Ryga looked for ways of using this material in other forms. Of the short stories included in the abortive "Poor People" collection, he subsequently found a place for three ("Betrothal," "A Touch of Cruelty," and "The

Wife of Sid Malan'') in his second published novel, *Ballad of a Stone-Picker*. He also incorporated one ("High Noon and Long Shadows") in the unpublished novel, "The Bridge." Four others, "Gold in the Aspens," "Love by Parcel Post," "Nellie-Boy," and "Half-Caste," are now seeing the light of day in *The Athabasca Ryga*, together with another very interesting early story on the theme of female repression and self-emancipation, "The Meek Shall Inherit," a tale with a message that will find many receptive ears nowadays but in 1960 when it was written was well ahead of its time. Its author was unable to find a publisher or broadcaster for it back then.[52]

Even after *The Athabasca Ryga* two of the "Poor People" stories will remain unpublished, although they may be consulted in manuscript form at the University of Calgary archives. They are "Legacy of the Meek" and "Brothers," two very interesting pieces in which Ryga arguably allowed his political purpose to overcome his artistic control as a writer. "Legacy of the Meek" describes two families' search for work and a better life in the Prairies and northern forests, and explores the "fate" that seems to dog one of them with continual ill-luck and misery. The story climaxes with a shocking scene of exploitation and violence at a sawmill, and ends with the victim, "Hard Times" Bill, refusing to take legal action against the owners of the mill. It is a tale that leaves a bitter taste in the mouth, and one can easily see why the CBC did not find it palatable in the early '60s, but it is a powerful piece of experimental writing that will, hopefully, eventually find a publisher.[53]

The same is true of "Brothers." Here two close friends, both young Ukrainian farmers, marry two sisters. They develop their farms in tandem, helping each other out and using exactly the same farming methods, and to start with they prosper. But they fail to adapt to changing times, and gradually slide back into poverty. They quarrel, each blaming the other for their distress, and, despite their wives' continuing friendship, live for decades in an atmosphere of mutual recrimination and hatred. A last chance for reconciliation presents itself, but the opportunity is lost, and the two men die together, bitter and alone. "Brothers" is a story that works on two levels. On the surface it is a study in human relationships, an exploration of the cantankerousness and stubbornness that comes over most of us from time to time, qualities that Ryga ruefully recognised as especially prevalent among the ethnic community from which he sprang. On another level it is an allegory of the Cold War, and Ryga, a member of the Canadian Peace Council, obviously intended it as a parable, a warning of what the Super Powers were capable of, given their record since World War II.[54] It was a theme to which he would return in later work, obliquely in his 1963 television drama "Two Soldiers," and directly in the controversial and much misunderstood masterpiece *Captives of the Faceless Drummer*.[55]

Meanwhile, in 1962, Ryga went back to the world of television drama, and quickly created two new TV scripts, "Storm" and "Trouble in Mind." Of these the first was accepted for broadcast by CBC Montreal, and the stage version is now published for the first time here. In addition, Ryga devoted part of 1962 to partially rewriting the novel *Hungry Hills*, a tedious activity that nonetheless proved worthwhile when the book was published by Longmans Canada the next year.[56] So when the year came to an end, the young author could look back on two major disappointments ("Poor People" and "Stone-Picker") but two triumphs, "Indian" and *Hungry Hills*. His career as a dramatist and a novelist had finally been launched.

WRITING AS A CAREER

The success of "Indian" plus the news that *Hungry Hills* had been accepted for publication confirmed Ryga's belief that writing was his vocation. The question now was how best to organize his life for that career. He knew that, in the early years at least, his income from writing would be meager. How, then, could he and his family exist financially while still allowing him to write full time? Norma offered to remain as the primary breadwinner, and as a result the Rygas decided to move to somewhere where their living expenses would be lower, and where they could be almost economically self-sufficient. They chose a large older house on a hillside near Summerland in the Okanagan. Here the climate was mild, the growing season long, and the opportunity for seasonal work in the fruit orchards abundant. George was a farmer by training and he loved gardening, so he would now become a horticulturist and grow most of the family's food. And when he wasn't gardening, he would write.

So in the spring of 1963 the Rygas moved to Summerland, British Columbia, to start a new life. Before leaving, George sorted through his old manuscripts and cast into the flames of a ceremonial bonfire all those that he regarded as juvenilia or first drafts. This may have been the time when certain novels, such as "Thy Sawdust Temples" and "Wagoner Lad" which are not to be found among the Ryga papers at the University of Calgary, vanished for ever. Be that as it may, the new British Columbia writer found he had plenty to do after settling in at Summerland. During 1963 he piloted *Hungry Hills* through the press, rewrote the novel "Old Sam," and began a new novel, "Men of the Mountain."[57] But although his dearest goal was to write another successful novel, he realized that his main chance of earning money by the pen was in the field of TV drama where he already had a reputation. That year he wrote nine new TV dramas: "Two Soldiers," "Bread Route," "Bitter Grass," "Masks and Shadows," "Goodbye Is for Keeps," "Chelkash," "For Want of Something Better to Do," "The Pear Tree," "The Tulip Garden," and two radio plays, "Ballad for Bill," and "Departures." At least eight of these eleven scripts were accepted by either CBC Montreal or CBC Toronto, and at least five of them ("Two Soldiers," "Bitter Grass," "For Want of Something Better to Do," "The Pear Tree," and "The Tulip Garden") were produced as TV plays, the others being transformed into radio dramas.[58]

Of the TV productions, the two most successful (and notorious) were the implicitly anti-war "Two Soldiers," which received very mixed reviews, and "For Want of Something Better to Do," which caused a minor political storm. George Ryga later remembered these exhilarating months, when his work was reaching a mass audience and provoking a response at the national level, in these terms: "Then came more TV plays: 'Two Soldiers,' a commentary on army life during times of peace; the uselessness, the rotting away of human beings . . . I took an original Gorky story ('For Want of Something Better to Do') and adapted it in a Canadian setting, which raised the ire of Diefenbaker in Parliament because he said things like that couldn't happen in Saskatchewan. Someplace else maybe, but not Saskatchewan . . ."[59] But it was the production of "The Tulip Garden" that meant the most to him personally, and the memory of this event was to influence his own decision on how to live with stomach cancer in 1987. He recalled the occasion in the following words:

> "Then I did a play on the immortality of the death ritual, called 'The Tulip Garden', with the late John Drainie playing the lead role. It was a very moving experience for me because in the story Drainie's wife had cancer and had been chopped up time after time and they had given her no dignity. She had to die in pieces. Well, when John took this role he knew he himself had terminal cancer. When I heard about his passing it came as one of those shocks that you get as a writer. You know, one can get used to increasing income, and one can get used to the politics of struggling with people who are going to battle you. But the thing a writer is faced with and which is difficult to reconcile is the fact that sometimes the people who work with you know more than you do about what they're doing. And they suffer more than you do. This has happened time and again. It happened with *The Ecstasy of Rita Joe*, where a woman actually called Rita Joe died in conditions very similar to those in the play . . ."[60]

By the end of 1963 Ryga's path as a writer was set. He would divide his time between radio and TV drama, the stage, and novels. Whatever the medium, he would write about real life, and especially the lives of the disadvantaged or outcast members of Canadian society. Most of his writings would be in some sense didactic, plays or books that had a purpose, a message. Many of his writings would be seen as political or in some other way controversial, and for this he would be frequently criticised and sometimes blacklisted. His method of writing, especially his approach to drama, would be experimental. Some experiments would work better than others, but they would all be interesting, almost always breaking new ground stylistically, conceptually, or in terms of content. *The Ecstasy of Rita Joe* would be his most famous play, "Grass and Wild Strawberries" his most wildly successful, *Captives of the Faceless Drummer* his most controversial, and *A Letter to My Son* his warmest and his own personal favourite. *Rita Joe* was a work that stirred a nation's conscience, and for a while after it was first produced in 1967 Ryga was something of a national celebrity. Naturally he received a lot of mail at the time, and one of the letters came from the Edmonton schoolgirl, Zoë Cope, who asked him to reply to a questionnaire she and her classmates were sending to famous Canadian writers. One question posed was the inevitable: "Why did he become a writer?" This introduction has been an attempt to describe how — and to some extent to explain why — George Ryga, farm boy from Deep Creek, became Zoë Cope's major Canadian writer. But it would be incomplete without the ex-farm-boy's own answer to the question in his reply to her:

> No single incident inspired me to write for a living.
> Writing is an outcry — a struggle for breath from the
> moment of birth. A child leaves a wiggly-jig in sand
> with a stick; a man or woman sit through a night,
> talking; and others make up songs to sing. It is all a
> record of man talking to God, requesting that his
> days on this earth be not without meaning. This is

what writing is in its purest form. All experiences affect my writing. Talking to you like this changes a scene in a play I will write tomorrow morning. My travels and impressions, bits of conversation overheard on bus or ship, a song on a transistor radio — this is life that hums through and over me, and later in my home I recreate and rearrange it as if in answer to some silent question I hear asked of me . . . The most admirable quality in a person, writer or book is to be ready to take on a fight, even if it brings you down on your knees at times. The curse of our times is complacency — where people retreat to their "little boxes on a hillside" — while on the other side of the earth enormous jets can shower death on the paddies of Vietnam and it makes no difference to us as we eat our three meals and turn on taps and switches for conveniences that seldom fail us. Life is conflict — we must ache, love, struggle — for out of this we begin the long climb from Animal to Man.[61]

THE ATHABASCA RYGA

The Athabasca Ryga is divided into six sections. The first section, this introduction, has included several short excerpts from George Ryga's writings, including extracts from *Beyond the Crimson Morning*, "The Bridge," and *Song of My Hands*, as well as from his nonfiction articles, interviews that he gave to reporters, and a talk he delivered to an academic gathering. Bibliographical details of these sources will be found in the endnotes to this introduction.

The second section, "Looking Back: Athabasca in Retrospect," presents two essays in which Ryga, at different points in his literary career, reflected upon and evaluated his childhood and teenage years in Richmond Park and Athabasca. "A Essay on *A Letter to My Son* was written in 1985. It is a concise and eloquent statement of some of Ryga's most deeply held political principles, and it is also a cultural manifesto, an appeal for a new and better kind of Canadian literature. Ryga praises the late Stan Rogers for successfully attaining as a songwriter one of his own fundamental goals as a playwright and novelist: the imaginative portrayal of Canadian folk-heroes as symbols that evoke the stoic courage and unsung achievements of ordinary working people. The essay is also revealing as a summary of Ryga's mature perspective on his ethnic heritage. He explains bluntly why he fled his parents' farm and temporarily turned his back on the Ukrainian language and culture. But he also recognises that another of his major tasks as a writer and as a Canadian has been to find a way to repossess honestly that heritage, to "take the best of what once was and carry it forward in the company of others to something greater."[62] In "Essay on *A Letter to My Son*" we are given a brief glimpse of a great Canadian writer pondering the big questions: the course of his early life, the significance of his past work, the relationship between literature and political change, and the objectives of his future writing.

"Notes from a Silent Boyhood" is an earlier, more genial and rhapsodic, collection of reminiscences about life as a schoolboy in Richmond Park and as a wage-labourer in Athabasca. It was written soon after the publication of *Ballad of a Stone-Picker*, and in the same year as *The Ecstasy of Rita Joe*. It might be described as a set of notes for the first chapter of an autobiography, a chapter centred on the themes of education and self-education. We learn about Ryga's teachers, about the wealth of literature they opened up for him, about his initiation into the politics of wage-labour, about his first steps as a writer, and about his departure from Athabasca to explore and confront "the world in upheaval over the horizon."[63] As an argument these notes are loosely organized, but as a sequence of images they possess that magical quality found in the best of Ryga's writing: the ability to call back from the past the sight, sound, and feel of people and places as they were originally perceived and experienced. That was an aspect of his craft at which George Ryga was especially gifted, and "Notes from a Silent Boyhood" is one of the most evocative pieces of nonfiction he has left us.

Ryga's talent for conjuring reality with words was already evident in the first full-length novel he wrote, the unpublished manuscript titled "The Bridge," excerpts from which comprise section three of this volume. Although he finished a complete first draft of "The Bridge," Ryga never revised it for publication. The extracts printed here for the first time are taken from the first half of the novel, and are presented in the same order as in the manuscript. They represent between one quarter and one third of the total work. Longer omissions are indicated by a centred bullet, smaller ones by ellipses.

The initial segments from "The Bridge" included here could be collectively titled "Memories of Richmond Park." The first scene recreates George's memory of his father as a blacksmith repairing a plough: a hard-working artisan, tired but strong, an awe-inspiring machine who would sometimes relax and turn momentarily into a warm and friendly human being. It is followed by other impressions of the farm and its inhabitants, animal and human, as perceived by a young boy one summer in the late 1930s. The third scene evokes the atmosphere of that homestead on a dark and windy August night, with its racing clouds, eerie moonlight and moving shadows, and the constant sound of the nearby river. Next come fragmentary reminiscences of friends, parents, and visitors to the farm, interspersed with the formative learning experiences of childhood in the country: sawing logs, fixing motors, fighting other kids, attending the one-room school, reading books, listening to adults talk and argue, attending the Catholic mission, and, last but not least, playing truant from school and incurring the wrath of both teacher and parents.

These scenes of rural life merge into images of Athabasca town: the boy's first visit to a restaurant and to the Wheat Pool elevator, his first job away from home in a turkey packing plant (actually the Athabasca Creamery), the loneliness of living in a boarding house, and the experience of a sojourn in the local hospital. Then comes the move to Edmonton, new but equally dreary lodgings, and a different but equally mindless

63

job at a co-op store warehouse. Adolescence in the city, poverty and joblessness, encounters with hobos and prostitutes, the awakening of sexual desire, and the aching disappointment of young love spurned: these are some of the feelings and incidents captured in the Edmonton segment of "The Bridge." Our excerpts from the novel end with Ryga's recreation of life in the Northern Alberta lumber camp, an experience he endured during the winter of 1954-55.

Section four, "Athabasca Images," consists of an essay, a reminiscence, and a short story. Each in a different way reveals something about the Athabasca region and its people. The essay "Smoke," written when Ryga was aged sixteen, was the work that won him his first scholarship to the Banff School of Fine Arts. "Smoke" is a tour de force, an account of pioneer life in Northern Alberta that is at once accurate, systematic, and, above all, wonderfully evocative. The first half of the essay deals with pioneer life on the eve of World War I, when most of the area around Athabasca was first settled. In the opening paragraphs Ryga relates the arrival of the first immigrants to Athabasca, their motives for coming, their initial sense of disappointment and discouragement, and their determination to stay notwithstanding the soul-destroying hardships and sorrows of the early years. He describes how they built their first log cabins, cleared their first patches of land, and struggled to make their oxen plough the virgin soil. He explains the pioneers' monotonous daily tasks: extracting tree stumps, picking stones, rolling boulders, ploughing, sowing by hand, harvesting, and threshing with a flail. He points out dispassionately the poverty that these tough, resolute men and women endured — their meagre possessions, inadequate clothing and implements, restricted opportunities for education — but also understands the joy and happiness they found in their close-knit families and their simple, self-reliant lives in daily contact with a natural environment they had grown to love.

The remainder of the essay traces the history of the pioneers through the 1920s, the setbacks of the Depression years, and the relative prosperity of the late 1930s when many of the farmers acquired tractors and automobiles. Ryga describes the building of schools and community halls, and the growth of cultural activities and political participation: the first stages of a process whereby a diverse group of Polish, Ukrainian, German, Scandinavian, British and French immigrants developed a common national consciousness and became Canadians. And he suggests, in conclusion, that by the eve of World War II these pioneer families were enjoying a measure of hard-won freedom and prosperity that they had never experienced in Europe. They had, in short, created something worth fighting for, which was why they responded to the call to save their old homelands from the scourge of fascism. "Smoke" thus ends on a patriotic note: in 1949 the young George Ryga was proud to be a Canadian, and he remained throughout his life a champion of Canadian culture and the Canadian ideal of a multicultural nation.

"The Pitchfork" is a vignette, a reminiscence about a Scottish neighbour for whom George worked as a day-labourer at hay harvest time. It is the longest of several such portraits in *Beyond the Crimson Morning*, and the one that best captures the atmosphere of farmwork in Richmond Park. The story recounts an accident that Ryga witnessed as a child, and its strength lies in its faithful depiction not only of the incident itself but of the character and reactions of the old man involved. Pride comes before a fall, but the victim of his own hubris endures his punishment with wry stoicism.

"One October Evening" is a darker work. It is an undated fragment, the opening of an unfinished short story which was probably begun by Ryga in the mid-1960s, but it stands on its own as a portrait of a town and of some of its inhabitants. The subject is also an accident, but this accident is fatal and the victim is an innocent Métis woman caught up in a routine of prejudice, sexism, and violence. Implicitly "One October Evening" asks the same questions as *The Ecstasy of Rita Joe*: why do these things happen, and how can they be stopped? The story can be read as a fine piece of writing, but it is more than that: its message remains relevant today since, regrettably, we have yet to find satisfactory solutions to the problems it identifies.

Section five of *The Athabasca Ryga* comprises five short stories: "Love By Parcel Post," "The Meek Shall Inherit," "Gold in the Aspens," "Nellie-Boy," and "Half-Caste." Four of these were included in the unpublished collection "Poor People" (1962) and remained unpublished thereafter, although Ryga did turn at least one, "Gold in the Aspens," into a radio drama. The fifth short story, "The Meek Shall Inherit," may have been the first fictional tale that he ever wrote, and it appears to be the only piece that he ever submitted for broadcast or publication under a pseudonym, Elgin Troy. Marital problems and the tortured nature of male-female relationships are the subject matter of the first three of these stories. "Love By Parcel Post" shows Ryga at his most genial. It is a warm and only slightly mocking account of a marriage arranged by mail, in which the subterfuges engaged in by each partner cancel each other out, and all ends happily. Ryga pokes fun at human foibles and conceit, but there is no anger or bitterness in this piece, only an implicit suggestion that none of us are perfect and that we would do best to honestly accept each other for what we are.

"The Meek Shall Inherit," on the other hand, is more of an accusation and a personal statement. Ryga is here denouncing a society which has no better way of caring for an orphan teenage girl than by forcing her into a loveless and degrading marriage with a lecherous old man. In particular his rebuke is directed at the clergyman who arranges the marriage and at the fundamentalist church that is not a house of worship but a compassionless court of moral judgment. The author's sympathies in the story clearly lie with the young girl, Brenda, and with the handicapped vagrant with whom she finds an hour of comfort and love. The last lines are a manifesto, and in retrospect we can see that "The Meek Shall Inherit," had it found a publisher when it was written, could have made a useful contribution to the literature of women's liberation that began to develop in the early 1960s. There may be less need now for its polemical message, but it is still worth reading as a sensitive study of a young woman's struggle for her own identity.

"Gold in the Aspens" is a "sad bitter tale."[64] It shares some similarities in theme and plot with "The Meek Shall Inherit," and was apparently based upon an real incident that occurred in Northern Alberta when Ryga was a child. His sympathies again lie not with the warped and barren institution of marriage but with the two brothers who dare to break society's rules, the first by his adulterous love for Polly and the second by his compassionate care for her and her land. Like "The Meek Shall Inherit," then, "Gold in the Aspens" champions sexual freedom against the fundamentalist Christian view that physical love outside marriage is a sin, and it challenges that traditional moral judgement as a dangerous form of prejudice, one that can have tragic results.

Prejudice and its consequences are the central themes of the two other short stories in this section. "Nellie-Boy" is a disturbing exploration of how callousness is born of fear and ignorance. Neither as a boy nor as a youth is the protagonist in the story evil; his unkind and intolerant actions are done mainly from frustration that the abnormal creature he has encountered refuses to act as he expects and demands. His brutality, Ryga suggests, is in part caused by social conditioning — he imitates adults and older kids — but in part it is a defensive lashing out at the unknown and the incomprehensible. The ending of the story pulls no punches — no reconciliation or even communication has been achieved — yet Ryga suggests a glimmer of hope: the bully knows his actions were wrong and is ashamed of them.

"Half-Caste" is also about prejudice, but this time racial. The story depicts with merciless clarity the unavailing struggle of an unmarried mother to create an independent life for herself and her young son, a struggle which ends with her decline into prostitution while he roves aimlessly around a city with other street-kids. She repudiates and he loses touch with the black man who tries to look after them from a distance. The boy's betrayal of his black father demonstrates not only the mindless cruelty of race hatred, but also the way in which well-meaning individuals may be trapped by peer pressure into acquiescing in it. Yet the message here, though harsh, is fundamentally optimistic. Prejudice, Ryga is saying, can be understood and can be overcome, if the will to do so exists.

The final section of the book prints for the first time two early dramas, "Village Crossroad," which was probably the first play Ryga ever wrote, and "Storm," which was written soon after *Indian*. "Village Crossroad" is a powerful and disturbing piece, an investigation of teenage gang violence and of the fatal attraction that this kind of machismo posturing has for some women. Its theme is also the cruelty of prejudice, in this case prejudice against the slightly malformed and simple-minded victim of a motorcycle accident. Harold, the protagonist, is torn between imitating the bullying ways of the gang-leader or following his own decent, but seemingly ineffectual, instincts in his wooing of the disdainful Margie. The young Ryga's faith in humanity is revealed in Harold's decision, but we are left uncomfortably aware that the outcome might well have been different.

"Storm" is a less violent and angry play, but it too deals in harsh realities: loneliness, fear, marital breakdown, the difficulty of communication, and the precariousness of human life. A city woman finds herself alone in an isolated farmhouse with her young son, where she anxiously awaits the return of a missing husband. A blizzard rages outside, and the woman is about to give birth to a baby she hopes may save her marriage, but it will also keep her imprisoned in a lifestyle she hates. Again Ryga provides an optimistic end to the play: if we so choose we may see the city woman, like Harold in "Village Crossroad," as an example of the unsung "nameless masses" that George Ryga later strove to make the heroes of a new kind of Canadian literature.

This, then, is *The Athabasca Ryga*: a collection of two plays, three essays, seven short stories, and excerpts from a novel Together they give a picture of the land where George Ryga grew up and the culture that helped form him as a writer and a thinker. I hope that readers of this book will learn something of value about George Ryga the human being as well as about George Ryga the writer, and will find that they can then return to his better-known plays and novels with an expanded perspective.

ENDNOTES

1. "Replies to a Questionnaire," unpublished manuscript, University of Calgary archives, p. 1; also, interviews with Nick and Nettie Evasiuk, Gene and Vi Kowalchuk, Anastasia Shalapay, and Mary Gislason (Athabasca, 1988-90).
2. George Ryga, quoted in Peter Hay, "George Ryga: Beginnings of a Biography," *Canadian Theatre Review*, #23 (Summer 1979), p. 39.
3. Interviews with Nick and Nettie Evasiuk, Anastasia Shalapay, and Mary Gislason (Athabasca, 1988-90); also information supplied to the Athabasca Archives by Mary Ryga and George Ryga, sen.
4. George Ryga, quoted in Hay, loc. cit., p. 39.
5. George Ryga, *Beyond the Crimson Morning*, Garden City, N.Y.: Doubleday, 1979, pp. 189-190.
6. George Ryga, "Notes from a Silent Boyhood," in George S. Opryshko (ed.), *Clover and Wild Strawberries: A History of the Schools of the County of Athabasca*, Athabasca, AB.: Alberta Teachers Association, 1967, p. 10.
7. "Replies to a Questionnaire," manuscript, p. 1.
8. *Beyond the Crimson Morning*, pp. 159-160.
9. "Notes from a Silent Boyhood," loc. cit., pp. 9-10.
10. George Ryga, "Essay on *A Letter to My Son*," previously unpublished manuscript of a CBC radio talk, p. 2.
11. George Ryga, quoted in Hay, loc. cit., pp. 39-40.
12. George Ryga, quoted in Hay, loc. cit., p. 40.
13. George Ryga, *Song of My Hands*, Edmonton, AB.: National Publishing, 1956, unpaginated.
14. George Ryga, quoted in Hay, loc. cit., p. 40.
15. George Ryga, interview in *Montreal Star*, 30th November, 1962. For this reference I am indebted to Jim Hoffman.
16. "Notes from a Silent Boyhood," loc. cit., p. 11.
17. George Ryga, "The Bridge," unfinished manuscript in the University of Calgary archives, pp. 37-39.
18. George Ryga, "Contemporary Theatre and Its Language," *Canadian Theatre Review* #14 (Spring 1979), p. 6. This article was delivered as a talk at the Learned Societies Conference held in Edmonton in May, 1975.

19. *Song of My Hands*, unpaginated.
20. *Song of My Hands*, unpaginated.
21. George Ryga, interviewed by Jerry Shack in, "George Ryga — Poet, Playwright, Novelist. A Special Interview," *The Ukrainian Canadian*, #514 (June 1969), p. 35.
22. George Ryga, quoted in Hay, loc. cit., p. 41.
23. "Notes from a Silent Boyhood," loc. cit., p. 11.
24. *Beyond the Crimson Morning*, pp. 57-59.
25. For this information I am indebted to Jim Hoffman. "Federico García Lorca" was also included in *Song of My Hands*.
26. *Beyond the Crimson Morning*, p. 56-57.
27. George Ryga, quoted in *The Ukrainian Canadian*, June 1969, p. 36.
28. "These Songs I Sing," unpublished manuscript, University of Calgary archives.
29. Fred Woods, *Folk Revival: The Rediscovery of a National Music*, Poole, England: Blandford Press, 1979, pp. 56-57.
30. For the information that Ryga met Lomax and MacColl at this time I am indebted to Jim Hoffman.
31. Hay, loc. cit., p. 43. Hay, however, is wrong to suggest that Ryga visited Scotland in 1955, and that he had not initially intended to go to Helsinki. According to Norma Ryga, attending the World Peace Congress was the primary purpose of George's first European trip in 1955-56. He visited Scotland, in part in order to do research on Robert Burns, on a subsequent trip in 1959.
32. George Ryga, "Rewi Alley, As I Knew Him," *Athabasca Echo*, 21 September 1956.
33. George Ryga, quoted in Hay, loc. cit., p. 44.
34. *Beyond the Crimson Morning*, pp. 17-20.
35. "My Song Is Still," *Song of My Hands*, unpaginated.
36. Information supplied by Norma Ryga.
37. Information supplied by Nick and Nettie Evasiuk.
38. "Prairie Wind," *Song of My Hands*, unpaginated.
39. "Federico García Lorca," *Song of My Hands*, unpaginated.
40. Information supplied by Jim Hoffman and Norma Ryga. Ryga's bicycle tour of Scotland is described (in fictionalized form) in "The Bridge."
41. George Ryga, quoted in *The Ukrainian Canadian*, June 1969, p. 36.
42. George Ryga, quoted in Hay, loc. cit., p. 42.
43. George Ryga, quoted in *The Ukrainian Canadian*, June 1969, p. 36.
44. George Ryga, *Night Desk*, Vancouver, BC.: Talonbooks, 1976. A 177 pp. manuscript with the same title, but differing extensively from the published novel, is in the University of Calgary archives. It dates from October 1960. Curiously, there seems to be some controversy over which hotel was the model for Ryga's fictional night-desk. Norma

Ryga recalls that he worked at the Selkirk Hotel, and that *Night Desk* was in fact the first novel he ever wrote. However, the manuscript of "The Bridge" appears to antedate that of the first version of *Night Desk* (which was, in any case, very thoroughly rewritten before its eventual publication); moreover Nick Evasiuk recalls Ryga as working at the York Hotel. It is, of course, possible that he was employed on different occasions at both hotels, and that he worked on both novels at the same time (1959-60).

45. Information supplied by Nick and Nettie Evasiuk and by Norma Ryga.
46. George Ryga, *Hungry Hills,* Toronto, Ont.: Longmans, 1963; revised edition, Vancouver, BC.: Talonbooks, 1974. Ryga's file cards about the six novels may be consulted in the University of Calgary archives, which also holds manuscripts of "The Bridge" and both versions of *Night Desk.*
47. Manuscripts of "Village Crossroad" and "Pinetree Ghetto" are held in the University of Calgary archives.
48. *Ballad of a Stone-Picker.* London: Michael Joseph, 1966. The two earlier drafts of this novel, "Recollections of a Stone-Picker" (1962) and "A Forever Kid" (1964) are held in the University of Calgary archives.
49. George Ryga, quoted in *The Ukrainian Canadian*, June 1969, p. 37.
50. *The Ecstasy of Rita Joe.* Vancouver: Talonbooks, 1970. *Sunrise on Sarah.* Vancouver: Talonbooks, 1973.
51. Manuscripts of the ten short stories to have been included in "Poor People" are held in the University of Calgary archives.
52. Ryga's card files, held in the University of Calgary archives, document his unsuccessful attempts to find publishers for "The Bridge" and "Poor People."
53. The manuscript of "Legacy of the Meek" is held in the University of Calgary archives.
54. The manuscript of "Brothers" is also held in the University of Calgary archives.
55. *Captives of the Faceless Drummer.* Vancouver: Talonbooks, 1971.
56. *Hungry Hills.* Toronto: Longmans, 1963; revised edition, Vancouver: Talonbooks, 1974.
57. Although the manuscript of "Old Sam" was not burnt by Ryga in the spring of 1963 since he revised it later that year, it has nonetheless disappeared. It does not appear to be among the University of Calgary archival holdings. However, "Men of the Mountain" (1963) and "Man Alive" (a major, unpublished novel completed in 1966), are held in manuscript form in Calgary.
58. Manuscripts of most of these radio and television dramas are held in the University of Calgary archives.
59. George Ryga, quoted in *The Ukrainian Canadian*, June 1969, p. 37.

60. George Ryga, quoted in *The Ukrainian Canadian*, June 1969, pp. 37-38.
61. "Replies to a Questionnaire," manuscript, pp. 1-2.
62. "Essay on *A Letter to My Son*," manuscript, p. 2.
63. ibid
64. "Gold in the Aspens," manuscript, p. 2.

LOOKING BACK:
ATHABASCA IN RETROSPECT

ESSAY ON *A LETTER TO MY SON*

We seem to have reached a time in our national evolution when ethnic rediscovery is fast becoming a secondary industry. Coffee-table editions of books abound in crafts, cookery, placenames, origins, etc., as well as real and partially imagined histories of immigration settlements in various parts of this country. There is nothing disruptive or disturbing in these publications; they are designed for middle-class consumers, or as cultural stepping stones to middle-class acceptability. In fact, if the sum total of ethnic culture was a bowl of soup or an article of clothing, they would be the final touch of cultural transition.

There are, of course, some ground rules for ethnic authenticity. One of these is to never, never refer to the outrages of the past, when railways and mining concerns imported labour by the shiploads. Muscle was all that mattered in this arrangement. The fact that these bundles of muscles had names, a brain, and the ability to rejoice and sorrow in passing through life to death, was of little or no consequence. One does not labour this in coffee-table editions of books dealing in ethnic origins. There are still some of us who remember a shocking photograph of Doukhobor women doing duty as draft animals, pulling a plow to break land on the prairies. But these reminders of who we were once are not part of the current pop preoccupations.

In the push for upward mobility within the social fabric, there is even a pecking order as to who is "real" ethnic and who is not. A new phrase, "block settlement," has entered into this lexicon. The block settlement immigrant appears to have higher status in the ethnic game than one whose origins were more homogenized in early towns and rural homestead communities.

Growing up in a Slavic community with the incongruous name of Richmond Park, I turned away from survival by ethnicity at an early time in my life. My reasons were simple: I functioned in another language. And the cultural catch-basin of the small community was a convenient receptacle for social resentments, which, once voiced, became passive and ineffectual. And easily led to victimization by transplanted shepherds of the body and the soul. Marriages, careers, choices of places to live, all these were influenced not by enlarging awareness, but by commonly shared limits to vision. I spoke the language, sang the songs, ate the food — even to this day I prepare ethnic food with some expertise — but I could not, even as a boy, follow the ever-narrowing route of spiritual oblivion. My world was not the world earmarked for museums. Life was too short, and there was the world in upheaval over the horizon. It was a decision which was fateful in my understanding of our country and its people. Take the best of what once was and carry it forward in the company of others to something greater. But do not apologize or pretend to a history tailored to fashions or new class pretensions.

Yes, we were noble, we were mean, we craved for the impossible, and sometimes we did terrible things to our children. We were all workers, struggling to create something worthy under predominantly bad management. We still do; and wonder why wisdom is such a scarce commodity among those we entrust with our destiny. Otherwise, why wars? And the inevitability of the poorest among us fighting and dying in wars. Why hardship and unemployment in the richest resource nation in the world? Why such poor and badly prepared information about the world undergoing dramatic changes by the hour? And why, in a time of abundant paper and film, such a pale understanding of ourselves and our real and mythological heroes?

It is a problem I struggle with constantly, facing it in placenames commemorating people, not on the basis of contribution to human betterment, but on the prestige of wealth or previous colonial service. I faced it growing up in the community of homesteaders whose mailing address was the name of a playground for British royalty and their entourage. I face it in the realization that the Canadian hero or heroine in literature, in theatre, music, and the other arts, has the same denominator as those of revolutionary societies in that these heroes and heroines emerged from the common people and await the mythmakers and balladeers to give them form, substance, and majesty. This is the challenge of our day.

It is a challenge well served by an artist I never met in his short lifetime, but who became a powerful voice in helping to shape the form of a people's culture; I refer to the late Stan Rogers, a man of remarkable insights, artistry, and temperament. With little patience for professional soothsayers, he created songs of theatrical dimension, elevating the despair of aging into poetry and creating monuments of passion. In other songs, using the language of common speech, he created heroes of the nameless masses in the ordeals of seamen in storms, of ordinary foot-soldiers battling against American expeditions into Canada, of a prairie farmer stoically facing the ravages of declining health and financial disaster, songs of recklessness and banditry revealing a profound compassion for victims of ignorance, or economic points of no return. There is much we can learn from his work, for his explorations were complex and butted against the doors and windows of political and moral concepts behind which we have too often taken shelter, to the detriment of further evolution of our cultural work.

I would wish that *A Letter to My Son* would be viewed not as an ethnic work, but as a work arising from ethnic origins. When my father first encountered this drama, he wept, and we both achieved a reconciliation we had never had before. But this is not the story of my father; it is the story of many mythical fathers who both reared me and expelled me from the bondage of wanting, but not knowing how to attain; of poetry that rang against iron clouds, of pathos approaching in a churning cloud of hailstones; of children who preferred to read about them in a coffee-table book rather than deal with them in the solitude and distant-eyed reality of retirement centres; of wheelchairs pushed nowhere by nurses with Walkmans in their ears. And yet, the spirit rises in surprising moments. Even as recently as a month ago a prairie farm family repaired, then donated, a tractor for shipment to Nicaragua, to help the campesinos in that beseiged land. Of pensioners surrendering small savings to aid famine victims in North Africa. A northern highway worker jeopardizing his job by publicly refusing to pledge archaic allegiance to the Queen of England. Growing resistance by northern native peoples, outnumbered and with scant resources, against the colonial practices of the central government in dealings with them. The individual dream fuses with the universal understanding that life without dignity and compassion is only half a life.

"If only I had the knowledge to reach out where I wanted to go in my lifetime," an aging friend of the family once told me, his eyes burning with tears. And another muscular friend, muscling his way through his first novel, said, "I will write you into the ground — you just watch me!" At such moments the heart rejoices, races with joy. It is not the potential success or failure of these thoughts that matters, it is the doing and the wanting to do. The self-sufficiency of spirit to turn the soil, write a novel, master a complicated machine, by these offsprings of the boatloads dumped on these shores for temporary employment, and then largely forgotten as they went on to forge a civilization — piecemeal, without guidelines, and without benevolence from those who could be benevolent in the national interest. You see, I know of no poem, song, or story celebrating our painful history being helped to life and availability by a grudging and pervasive mentality that, to this day, regards the soup kitchen as the ultimate expression of Christian charity from those who have towards those who have not.

The same mentality still fosters difficulty in training our children in both our official languages; that is prepared to debate for generations land claims of our first peoples with little intention of settling these historic outrages against reason and against justice. In all this, in all the private and not-so-private thoughts of ordinary people about restraint programs, cruise missile tests, and new military installations on Canadian soil, new metaphors emerge. First come the cartoonists, with comments for the day; later the singers and poets will engrave in the mind a long-lasting statement of common consensus. In this there is optimism. It is a process worthy of the poet Stephanson, of Stan Rogers, of all to whom people matter, regardless of origin, language, or skin colour.

NOTES FROM A SILENT BOYHOOD

I was born, raised, and to some degree educated in Richmond Park — a small community north of Athabasca. In cold, pertinent facts this is possibly all that links me to my silent boyhood. In light of all that has happened in the intervening years, the statistics might seem even less important. For I was in formal school only seven years of my life. All that I learned in those seven years an average student today can master in less than one year of study. These are the facts — the pure statistics. Behind the facts are the plants of a million seeds that have sprouted and borne fruit.

My teachers, and who knows where they are now? — the Tkatchuks, the Brians, Staffords, and Kowalchuks — they occupy in my education the same significance as those other teachers I was to meet in my silence: Byron, Keats, Shelley, Burns, Dickens, William Morris, Walt Whitman, Karl Marx, Shakespeare, Goethe, William Carlos Williams, Hikmet, Ehrenberg, and the magnificent Nikos Kazantzakis! Seven years is a short time. Yet today it is a long, long while to take hold of the key through which the universe might be opened. I listened to Mahler the other night and heard a phrase of music so beautiful that tears of joy sprang to my eyes involuntarily. Yet it took Mahler over forty years of his life to create those three seconds of pure beauty and truth. How short is life — how long the road to our possibilities as human beings!

Before I went to school my vision was reduced to most of what I could touch, taste, smell. Rubber footwear mouldering in the sun, sour mud after a northern rain, the touch of newly turned earth, the acid-scent of poplar leaves and the steel-coldness of winters whose presence was felt the greater part of each year. Bread baking and split wood, sweating horses, smoke and kerosene, clover and wild strawberries — the coarse touch of tamarack wood, cruel as the arguments of cursing men who were always on the edge of violence, for the poverty was incredible and patience an unpredictable pool of water over which a storm always threatened.

I was born nearer to feudalism than the electric light bulbs of Edmonton, although Edmonton was only one hundred and twenty miles distant. And because the medieval blood flowed thick in my veins, the hawks and swallows of the dark ages wrestled early within my skull. At six I reached a higher elevation of religious sensitivity and revelation than any adult human I have since spoken to. Yet I stuttered — I had no words with which to describe profundities I had difficulty understanding twenty-five years later. I could neither read nor write. I was silent and alone, for every sensation and experience was my own with no influence or direction, for I was a child born out of context in time and space. I did not know this then — only in recent years have I seen with growing clarity the stumbling and inevitable course my life had to take for my work to ever make a reckoning with itself.

Men beat their livestock and their women — men and women sang and embraced at weddings and after a good harvest. I drank in the warmth of love, learned the songs that come with the blood at the mother's breast. If the words faltered, it mattered little, for I could create words later — it was life that was all-important — the deep roots drinking ice and nectar out of the earth. Sounds of sleds slapping the frozen roads — the child lost on the steppes — references to acacia and linden, the trees of love and stability — were planted into me in a land of stark forests and cold muskegs.

They taught me well — your teachers. What a difficult student I was, and how well they taught me!

"Good morning . . . thank you . . ." The words took weeks to learn. How wild and strange my hand was as I worked to master and print in straight lines with some legibility the twenty-six letters of the English language that would one day release me from the silence enforced upon my forefathers by centuries of persecution at the hands of kings and barons and priests! The letters came as the down on the breast of a gosling; the letters came as iron claws pulling apart the clouds for the north American sun to shine through . . . . "The sky is blue today . . . the sky is blue today . . ."

Your teachers were the same children of circumstance that I was — only they were older by a few years. My first teacher guided my hand and my mind out of childhood even during that first year. "*D*, as in dog. *E*, as in everlasting life . . . I am a teacher because I have not got resources to become anything else. I am a political man. I believe we are all brothers and sisters. If one of us hurts, no matter where in this world, we must all feel the pain . . ."

He taught me to read and write. He taught our community how to organize and direct their grievances so they might be heard. For this he was betrayed and forgotten, for even before I finished school at Richmond Park, he was forbidden to teach in Alberta and his career as a teacher came to an end. But I, the hungry young animal, forgot him as well, for I was spanning generations with each year I spent in that drafty log building with the warping floors and the gasoline-barrel heater, listening but seldom hearing the droning new teacher with frayed cuffs and chalk stains on the shiny seat of his trousers. Sometimes I stared into the face above me — an ashen face crying out for the outdoors and the sun of summer; crying out for acceptance in the community, for love and children of his own. A face I could sadden with disobedience and indifference, which I often did. For he was in the nineteenth century, pulling me, resisting and uncooperative, out of the seventeenth century.

One of the teachers played a piano at recess in her teacherage. I dropped the ball I held and listened to the music that fell as water over pebbles, and it conjured up a vision of a day yet to come, when I sat on a stack of lumber munching bread and sausage and listening to my father and another man talking with the ribaldry excited by food and comradeship. And as I ate I stared into the town of Athabasca for the first time and thought to myself, my God, what a beautiful city!

Then came the devouring restlessness, when my tongue stuck to the roof of my mouth. I was hungry for words — the miles and miles of pages I was to read later on. And I was afraid of the numb, slow death overtaking those around me. I learned quickly, and then I could neither hear nor see what was wanted of me in the school. The teachers spoke to me, and the inspector of schools spent a morning with me. They let me complete the final two years in that last winter, and my schooling in the transitory buildings that listed and decayed even as we sat in them, ended. The abrupt, final break, sharp as the caw of a crow. Also, the end of my life in Richmond Park, for though I remained a few years longer in the community, my destinations were being drawn, even against my will at times.

We all who left school that summer took the bridle of a horse attached to a stoneboat and led the horse down to a grey-soiled field over which burned a pale northern sun. We had become men, given our sword of manhood and told to turn our faces into the hot winds of our private and many wars.

Some of us went to work in the mills, even though we were all below the minimum industrial age. I groped and struggled, on my own without compass or rudder, reading everything from mail-order catalogues to classics to love-story magazines, an over-ripe young woman who often visited our house left for me. I could never digest enough.

Then one day I was working on a scaffold beside Dave Stirling, who talked to the men on the construction crew, some twice his age, as if they were his own children. He explained to me the mechanics of reinforced concrete and of expansion ratios of various construction materials. But I was in another world, driven by other forces that were giving me no comfort. He touched my chin with his fingers. "Slowly . . . speak slowly. Take a week or a month, but say it clearly."

Then he gave me books and newspapers that explained and took sides on great issues of the day, and all the parts began falling into place. The first contact with Byron made the heart sing:

> The mountains looked on Marathon
> And Marathon looked o'er the sea,
> Standing there an hour alone
> I dreamed that Greece might still be free!

I spent evenings with him and Ruth, who was later to become his wife. I loved them both with a depth I had never before experienced. What a loss it was to have them leave my life even as I was leaving the place of my birth.

On a stump in the woods I wrote my own first words on that which was nearest to me — a close horizon that was both home and a stifling prison, for the world was wide and the ocean was great, and I had to see them all. My teachers were there with every word I wrote, and they taught me well, for I won out against hundreds of others who were trained in the best city schools on the prairies. With a cream cheque in my pocket and an oversized jacket on my back . . . — ". . . The boy will grow . . ." — I left.

I left for Banff and my first view of the mountains. I left for many places around the world, leaving behind me a path strewn with poems and songs, stories, plays and books. The silence ended. The long argument with God had begun, for I am not content to spend my life entirely as a fool. And for every breath of air given me, I have had to pay penance with ever-deepening seasons of brooding loneliness and introspection when a man's soul turns in on itself in search of truth and meaning to all existence, of which his own is but a minor part. Each groping step keeps taking me from the mire and tangleweed of half-life through the hurly-burly jazzy star-explosions and splitting cobblestones by arc-light of the great cities — London, Paris, Moscow, Los Angeles — around which the earth revolves as a wheel about its axis.

I kiss and embrace the revolutionary, for his is the eternal half of the human will! I hold in my hands the kneeling man planting a tomato bush, for he speaks to God as wisely as an astronaut, flying into the eye of heaven! I sing the jingle-jangle songs of today's children, for they are more beautiful than we might ever have been! I breathe deeply the growl and hum and bangle of life, for it redeemed me from the silent despair that once threatened me.

CHILDHOOD MEMORIES: SELECTIONS FROM "THE BRIDGE"

. . . He was a boy on his father's farm, straining his eyes for a distant fence. A wind stirred, and an entire field of clover in blossom bowed. Clouds flecked the heavens, and shadows swept the clover and farm buildings in the wake of the wind.

"Come here, boy!" And he followed the voice into the shed. "Help me with this."

He took the bellows handle from his father, and worked it up and down. The fire in the smithy showered sparks to the ceiling, and then hissed into a constant blue flame. A heavy, knotted hand picked up a long set of pincers, which opened and gnawed on the plowshare, raising it, and torturing its bent point into the fire. He thought he heard the steel moan, as licks of flame wound around it and turned orange. A delicate feeling of strength and mastery warmed his spine. The flames leaped higher, and a low growl rose through the shed . . . . "Hey! Slow down, or you'll be burning down the ceiling! I just want the point heated red-hot," the pincers said, as they reached out with their jaws and tapped the blunt edge of steel in the fire.

"Okay, Dad." A squirrel twittered over the sound of his industry. He wanted to drop the bellows handle, and rush out to follow the squirrel . . . to scare it into sitting up and facing him angrily. To throw a stone against the board fence and see the little animal bolt into the garden or some other avenue of escape.

•

The pincers bit the tail of the plowshare and with the angry sweep of a puppy shaking a rag doll, threw it against the blue anvil. The defiant red glow hissed on the oiled iron and spat orange stars of anger into the air. The crash of the hammer made the boy jump. He watched in fascination and horror as the hammer lifted. The steel point had flattened and darkened under the impact, but now it recovered its glowing life, and again crisp particles of life crackled off its surface. The second and subsequent blows killed the steel, and it followed the thundering demands of the hammer, stretching out like a dying animal, and pointing and bending its nose slightly over the edge of the anvil. Then it was left alone. The pincers and hammer fell to the floor of the shed in exhaustion. The plowshare exhaled a breath of pale blue smoke. His father blew a puff of air and wiped his temples, then turned to open a drawer in a wall and run his hands through tinkling bolts and scraps of iron.

The boy looked on the cracked and dusty pine floor, until his eyes came to rest on the heels of his father's shoes. They were twisted and cracked heels, worn equally on the outside edge, so that the denim pantleg touched only the inner part of the shoe. His eyes went upward and he saw the lower back leg pushing against the trouser. Then up to the small but perfectly rounded buttocks, with the two square, close-fitting pockets dirtied and worn at the flaps. The shirt billowed out over the belt and stuck to the shoulders where dark, great patches of perspiration glued the cloth to the body.

•

Chickens always fled before the rain. A gust of wind would turn the hens over on their sides, where they clawed at the air in an effort to upright themselves. Then another gust would roll them on their feet, and they would run with their necks outstretched. He would jump in the way of the fleeing birds and shoo them back into the wind. But they squawked terribly and ran between his legs.

Hungry pigs ran as anxiously to the feeding trough at six o'clock in the evening. He rode one once, holding on to its ears. And it squealed but made no attempt to throw him off. The pigs ate greedily. He wanted to cut a hole in the side of its stomach for the mash to come out. He wanted to see if it would eat forever without realizing it was being cheated.

. . . Hungry men did not say much when they ate, and then talked too loudly and smiled too widely when they had finished.

Men in black clothes were missionaries.

Big boys smoked behind the barn and drew sketches with a stick in the dust of the lower parts of women with no clothes on. They always scolded and chased away smaller boys who wanted to see. Girls had too much hair . . . .

And you had to step carefully over twigs and branches in the woods, for they might suddenly spring out to great lengths and pierce through your bare feet.

A dirty kitchen made him hungry, and the sound of a gurgling stream made him want to pee.

He wanted to pick up all the soil a plough turned over and throw it up to scent the whole world.

Nobody walked all the way up a road, or he would get lost and never return.

Strawberries had the best taste of anything, and both ends of a caterpillar cut in two wriggled away from each other . . . .

A summer day lasted forever, and nobody could live through it without going to sleep.

Lightning made someone very angry, and seagulls never died . . . .

•

The low wind of an August night, blowing across the garden

from the house to a haystack where he would bed down to sleep. Like the aged dying by a roadside, the viny hands of pumpkins reached into the hollows and rises of the earth and perished, stretched across as much land as they could reach. There was something terrifying about their limpness and blackness in the night. The wind blew through the moist, dark, shredding leaves of the sudden frost — the very tragedy of life in rising defiantly, and then falling before the first savagery of the elements.

The river mourned the autumn, too. Where once the moon danced off the flickering surface of the water and jumped back for the sky, now the swollen, pensive waters devoured sullenly the faint light from the heavens. Death was in the air, and he was frightened . . . .

•

> The highwayman came riding, riding,
> The highwayman came riding,
> up to the old inn-door . . . .

And the night became a cover of romance and gallantry. Clouds were silhouetted against the iron sky. The puffs of vapor spread and compressed as they were pushed across the dome of heaven by the wind. He could see indistinguishable forms changing into faces of animals and men, and then they became distorted into forms remembered by the memory of the ages, but no longer recognizable to the eye of reason. Elation swept through him, and he wished his birth had been swept back into antiquity so he might have chronicled Hannibal or known Jesus Christ by first name . . . .

A thundering group of mounted riders came over the brink of the horizon and crossed the hills toward him. He had to look up as they came near, for they blotted out the moon and stars on their dark mounts and pulled the clouds apart with their upraised arms as curry-combs through fine wool. He fell backwards and the riders came over him in an endless line, hooves pounding over his chest and stomach, and driving him deep into the earth . . . . He stirred and struggled to rise out of the depression in the hay in which he slept.

He rose to his knees and peered over the edge of the stack and across the liquid fields. The wind brushed his hair up and over his head, and the coldness felt pleasant to his hot cheek. The wind caressed his neck and hummed songs in his ears, the music rising in volume when he turned his face directly into the current and his earlobes caught the full force of the moving air.

He looked towards the house, grey and gaunt in the moonlight. Windows were dark pits in the face of the building, and a cat curled into a ball lay in front of the door. Long stalks of morning-glories, frozen and pinned to the eaves, wrestled and nudged each other.

The river was constant and cold. A log floated by, and it rolled and turned like a balloon. It seemed bloated, and it gleamed like ice under the moonlight. He watched in fascination as it moved past. Then he gasped. For the driftwood hit a slight whirlpool, and in twisting threw out one branch on the surface of the water. It was a thick branch cut sharply a short distance from the trunk. It reminded him of the amputated arm of Fred, the countryside idiot. The entire log appeared to live suddenly, and to resemble the weak-brained man, as if he were floating on his back, his feet close together, his good arm behind and underneath him, and his other ghastly stump of arm reaching out blindly to clutch for help with fingers and forearm whose loss he could never completely comprehend. The form drifted on, and was lost behind some overhanging willows.

He jumped up and slid off the stack. The blow of the ground racing to meet him was surprisingly hard, and his sleep-weakened knees bent under him, and he fell on his side. He looked up to see a lizard-shaped cloud quickly cover a grin on the moon. He felt terribly lonely and cold, and rising to his feet, he began running to the house.

The pumpkin vines reared and curled around him, dragging

93

him to the ground. He screamed, but the wind plucked the sound off his lips and threw it against the poplar trees, breaking it into little fragments.

. . . An oil lamp seemed searingly close to his face suddenly and he bolted back into the mattress.

"Now what the hell were you doing in the garden at this hour?" he heard his mother say. Her face was deeply shadowed, and her white hair softened the light and made the room gentle and close. She bent down to kiss his lips and left him. He covered his head, and lying on the top-end of the cover, tightened it with his toes. Then he ran his forefinger back and forth across the coarse, taut cloth. It made a pleasant, soft sound, like sleep being poured into a wooden box. A mosquito whined under the covers with him, but he made no attempt to find and destroy it.

•

Summers went and autumns came. Schoolbells always rang when the fun was best, and his father sent him to bed when he least wanted to sleep. He held to the end of a Swedish saw and it was pushed and pulled too far at a stroke by his father. Blocks of wood made a small pile from a log which two men could not lift when it was still uncut. An airplane in the sky made geese run for cover, and he liked the games of small calves and colts . . . .

Sometimes his father and mother became very friendly and washed dishes together. He was afraid of this friendship, for he became a stranger to them on these days. After they worked together, they would leave him alone and go into their bedroom together, and he would hear them rocking their bed. When they came out, they were always smiling, but his father never stayed in the house long. He would go out and split wood or cut trees with an axe and clear land. His mother baked and fed him cookies until his stomach pained . . . .

The boy across the road had a hare-lip and talked with a sound which reminded him of a church-bell ringing. Other children in the school would mimic him by saying "Mya, Mya" in the same moaning voice he spoke in. But he was a good friend, and the two of them would fight others together. Once they hurt a boy whose nose was always running. The boy tattled, and the teacher aimed a yardstick from one to another, as a hunter who cannot make up his mind which duck to shoot first. Both of them became upset and began crying, but the yardstick continued moving from one to the other. Then the teacher put the stick down.

"Stand up, both of you!" he ordered. One of the glasses in his spectacles was cracked, and divided his eye in two pieces. "Salute the flag!"

They both raised muddy and trembling hands to their heads and faced the flag. It fluttered on the wall, for a wind blew in behind it through a crack. A robin chirped outside and grasshoppers went "crick, crick . . . "

Sunlight from the open window warmed his shoes.

And his shoes were cold when the teacher ordered them to take their seats again.

•

. . . He was riding a cattle truck away from the farm. His shirt was shingle hard from starch, and his washed pants hurt him between the legs where they were tight. A woman who looked like his sick aunt welcomed him to the mission camp. She wore black with a white ring around the hood over her head.

"Are you cold, ma'am?" he had asked. They all laughed and he tried to hide behind the big wheel of the truck.

A man dressed like the woman, but with no hood over his bald head took his arm and pulled him out. "I'm Father McManus, and this is Sister Gertrude," he said, and smiled. Gertrude . . . the name made him think of hard pebbles which hurt through a shoe. He sang in the choir and she waved a baton in front of his face. Why didn't Aunt Margaret wave a baton and make boys sing? . . . she was too sick . . . .

"Holy Mary, Mother of God, pray for us sinners — now and at the hour of our death, Amen."

"Don't rush, boy. Don't rush. Think about what you say. The ball game won't start until you're finished . . . so don't rush . . ."

He stole a pie from the kitchen, and Father McManus caught him and made him wash his car with cold water.

He went to confession and told on three of the boys who jumped out the window to play at night. Father McManus reached out through the slot in the wall and pinched his ear for tattling.

A man on a motorcycle talked to him, and came to visit often after. He gave him a book of Arabic poetry, and the book made him think of pictures. When he had the measles, he drew a picture of a tree with a man lying on the grass beneath it, reading books and drinking wine.

The motorcycle brought his friend, who laughed. "For nine hundred years they've been painting that picture, and for a thousand years more they'll continue doing so."

He felt discouraged. There was so much to know, and who could teach him fast?

•

The first time his father took him into a restaurant, they had raisin pie and coffee. He looked about him. Long-haired farmers were sitting everywhere, eating raisin pie and drinking coffee. Those who had finished eating were smoking store-made cigarettes, flattened from the pressure of their hard, horny fingers. The waitress had a green stain on the belly of her apron. A lanky young fellow got up to leave. He paid his bill to the waitress, and left saying, "Don't take no wooden nickels . . ."

They went to the Wheat Pool grain elevator in the evening. The elevator operator was very fat and loud voiced. He drank beer some farmers had bought him to assure a better chance on their grading. They were sitting waiting to find what moisture content the wheat boiling in oil over a nearby burner contained.

"If my tractor don't work, I smack it with a hammer," a wild-eyed Swede, drunk and poor, said.

"Yeah — you smacked your way through three tractors in two years. How long before you go bust?" asked his neighbour, who wore a green shirt and red tie.

A truck drove up, and everybody scrambled to hide their beers behind empty paper boxes. A dog barked, and a guttural voice said, "Fuck you . . ."

He took walks in the evening, and dreamed the thoughts of rain against a window. Somewhere behind the trees, a John Deere tractor pounded a hymn of labour into a fast gathering night. Autumn skies were always so pensive. To the east, a leaden sheet spread over half the heavens. But to the west where the sun had gone down the rim of the earth was on fire, devouring the clouds, and becoming blue with orange cushions where it met the east. He walked and looked up and often stumbled. He wished never to sleep again, but walk far away or ride a horse like a cowboy in a lonely song. His thighs ached from a day of stooking, and he wondered if crutches made it easier to stand.

•

The last day at school was sunny and sleepy. Squirrels and woodchucks raced along the rail fence and chirped and screamed crazily. Tony, from across the creek, put up his hand with three fingers extended, signifying he wished to go to the outdoor toilet. He also put up his hand for the same purpose, and the teacher let them both go. Once outside, they found a ball and started to play catch.

Twenty minutes later, the teacher came out after them, and brought them both in by the ears.

He strapped them both in the basement, and altered their report cards to fail them together. They went home at lunch, and the shutter of boyhood closed on him in that last two-mile walk.

His mother wept, and his father cuffed him around the ears until he fell into bed, dizzy and tearful.

"When I die," spoke the burning eyes through wild, excited hair, "You will die of starvation like a beggar in the wilderness! You good-for-nothing!"

•

He learned to take motors apart, clean them, and reassemble the parts to work properly. He learned to drive a car with no brakes and a stripped first gear. He could dance a waltz, and by moving his feet faster could work his steps into a fox-trot. He could read a book upside down. He worked in the garden, hoeing away at his shadow until it shortened under him to be covered with one scratch at the dirt. And then the shadow lengthened in the other direction, and he learned to tell time by it. When he stood upright, and could see his neck beneath the head of the shade, it was time to go indoors and have a glass of tea. He awaited night . . . begged the earth to send it quickly to meet him so he might rest.

Before bed, he would meet the hare-lip on the road, and they would twist themselves a cigarette and smoke it together. The hare-lip stole tobacco from his father. They rolled the cigarette in brown wrapping paper, and it smelled and tasted like burning cloth.

•

"When they ask you, you tell them you're eighteen years old, do you hear?"

The foreman walked away and one of the workmen spoke bitterly, "Wish he'd shut his mouth a little more, or spit before he talks — you need an umbrella to talk to that guy!" The fine spray of spittle drifted across a ray of sunlight from an open window, and crates rattled as they were tossed on piles in the cool shed.

He returned to his bench. A stack of turkeys had accumulated, as the Mètis boy Dickie methodically sorted, weighed

and pinched each bird, then tossed them on separate branches in order of grades. His job was to wrap the heads of the
grade B's. They had been slaughtered carelessly, and dry blood
stuck to the beaks and necks. He had repeatedly cut his fingers
on the stiff wax wrapping paper, designed in neat triangle
sheets which, if wrapped properly about the heads of the birds,
could be tucked in just about the neck and would not come
loose in the various other steps of processing before ship-
ping. But even though he had cut his fingers in his work
many times, he could no longer tell where the cuts were, for
the odd bird had thick blood in its beak, and these birds had
stained his hands until his own blood became one with the
other. His eyes ached in the dim light, and his back tortured
him from constant bending over the bench. But there was no
complaining, for the shed contained one man who issued orders
and a dozen others who responded. He was one of those who
responded.

There was a man who assembled crates from ready-cut
lumber. He was old and bony, and his back had a perpetual
bend. One hand was flexible and fine, and in this hand he held
the nails. The other hand was bony and arthritic and handled
a hammer as if it were carved onto the wood handle. He let
go of the hammer only at mealtimes, and then he would put
the damaged limb into his trouser pocket.

The foreman was red faced and puffy. He breezed through
the building, shaking a fistful of order papers and taking all the
workmen in at one glance. "Come on! Come on! Let's speed
it up . . . we've got twenty crates to ship off tonight!" he
spoke to the far door, which he approached and kicked open
as he went through.

Night time . . . Mrs. Malkin kept a boarding house where
he stayed. She fed her boarders pork and beans, with different
hot and cold meats on various days of the week, except
Friday, when they got jackfish. For dessert, they had rice pudding and tapioca on alternate days. He ate the pudding, but

would not touch the main course, for it was turkey, and visions of paper-wrapped beaks with crusted blood on the necks passed before his eyes, nauseating him.

"What a pretty fellow, and he won't eat. Now what's the matter, my little tiddly-winks?" All the boarders were *tiddly-winks*. She had a bedroom below his, and at night, he heard laughter and muffled cries of "Oh, tiddly-winks! You beastie, you!" and more laughter. He found the laughter comforting, and would sleep on dreams of cranes beating the clouds of an autumn evening with their great wings.

He wrote letters to imaginary friends when he couldn't sleep and had to wile away the hours into weariness.

"My dear friend — How weary and dismal is life. Could I but lie by your side again and talk to you of the squirrels which came to my cabin the past summer, I would be so happy to have you listen . . ." He wrote once. Then he tore up the letter in a fit of shame, for he had no friends, and the cabin and squirrels were nonexistent. He wondered how one went about visiting the landlady's room. He longed to be called "tiddly-winks," and to be laughed at pleasantly. Maybe she would even let him sleep near her bed on the floor. He felt homesick, and wanted the severe face of his mother near his to kiss him on the cheeks as she always did. He tried to think of his father, but the effort tired him, and he dozed holding his head in his arms on the desk.

The terrible wrath of his foreman when he was caught pinning a "Grade B Poultry" tag on the coat of a townswoman who had come directly to the plant to purchase her Christmas fowl.

"Do that again, you little bugger, and I'll pack you in with those turkeys and ship you off . . ." He had to apologize to the woman, and he felt deeply humiliated.

A stormy winter . . . and he stood outside shops in his free hours, peering at merchandise distorted by heavy ice on the shop windows. A pair of loggers' boots amused him. Through

100

the overhang of ice, the toes of one boot seemed distended like footwear in a Lil' Abner cartoon. His view of the other boot was reversed, and he fancied he saw the toes coming to a delicate point.

. . . Snow sweeping up the street, and men meeting the icy gusts with their backs and upturned collars . . . .

There were dances for the young, but he only went to look and sit. He knew so few people, and those who came were with friends, so he felt like an intruder. Mornings, the sun would pour into his window, heralding Spring and the warmth of earth and sky . . . .

His parents came to see him once in a while, and they bought him dinner and took him to a movie. And always for the first hour with them he felt uncomfortable and lonelier than ever. He had begun to forget the names of cattle on the farm, and sunrises and breezes about the winter haystack seemed like memories from a fast fading past.

•

He was sent up a stepladder to change a burnt-out lightbulb once. He stumbled on the ladder and grabbed with his hand at the naked wiring. The building danced around him and the walls appeared to strike him from all sides at once. When he picked himself off the floor, his entire one side was numb, and the palm of his right hand was badly burned. The foreman directed him to the washroom to clean and dress the burn. He returned to work, and that evening was admitted to hospital with an infection.

The hospital had whitewashed walls and small, deeply set windows which looked out into a wall of dying spruce trees. His bed was near a west window, and he spent the first evening peering through the trees into the valley where the town lay. The air was frosty, and through the icy haze the lights magnified and glowed comfort into the wilderness.

"Electricity is warmer than a human heart," the doctor was beside his bed, "How's the hand, son?"

The man next to him was praying. His lines came out halt-ingly, for he had forgotten the prayers long ago, and was mak-ing up phrases to fill in where traditional ones were lost to him. He had a 100-watt lightbulb burning between his legs, for he had a genital disease and required constant heat. He was dying, and not being in particular pain, he feared death, for it promised no comfort. So he moaned and prayed, and made nights a living hell for his companions.

Somewhere in the building, a woman screamed in childbirth, and the praying face looked up in bearded wonder.

All eight men in the ward lifted themselves on their elbows and listened. A nurse walked in and turned off the bare overhead light. The door closed, and eight intent faces, raised above their pillows, became imprinted in the mind's eye through darkness as the woman screamed again.

"Our Father, who art in heaven . . ."

"Hey! The nurse forgot my sleeping pills!"

"What's wrong with you that you gotta have sleeping pills?"

"I've got a hole in my ass that won't heal, that's what . . ."

"Forgive us this day our daily sins . . ."

Still the stars of the town gleamed, and looking out he felt their light warming his face through the flickering, inconstant frost.

•

His dog had chased a coyote across a field of crusted snow by moonlight. There was much yelping and fury in the chase. The dog was fleet footed and thin, and soon overcame the wild animal. He had watched through a window, and when the dog was about to pounce on the coyote, the other animal suddenly turned over on its back and began fawning helplessly. The dog was bewildered.

"Sic him, Skip . . . come on, boy . . . Get him!" he urged softly. But the coyote succeeded, and soon both the dog and the scavenger were frisking about, and the game of death had become a ballet of new-found friendship. They criss-crossed the path of the moon, and there was a fierce beauty in their play . . . .

A nursing aide named Polly made his bed, and he smiled at her. She smiled back, and he felt happier. She brought him some magazines later and stayed to talk to him. She was freckled and had a large red birthmark on her left temple.

Days and weeks hurricaned away, and Polly's birthmark was remembered, but her face was lost in lapping waves of the river as it flowed over his life and made all memory translucent and suspended in liquid depths of discarded experiences.

He was given a transfer to the big Co-op store in the city, and one summer's day he packed a small valise of clothes and took the evening bus over the twists and bends of an unknown road . . . .

·

The small hotel room smelled of old cloth and paint. He lay awake at nights and listened to the deranged woman next door playing "potatoes." She would bring a bag of potatoes into her room in the evening, painstakingly peel them, and after she had peeled five pounds or so, she would pick out the peelings and attempt to dress each potato with exactly the same peel she had removed. Another game which seemed to delight her considerably was playing checkers, with her right hand playing against her left. She was pleasant and well liked, for she never walked past another guest in the hallway without stopping to speak a few words.

The personnel manager called him into the office from the warehouse for a conversation. He was a small man who squinted and went into long silences, during which he rested his chin in his left hand while he tapped a staccato rhythm on his desk with the fingers of the other hand. His desk top held a photograph of himself and a stack of Mickey Spillane books.

"Are you happy here, my boy? Do you ever think of coming into the office and working at a desk job, my boy?"

A long silence and his active hand turned into a three-legged horse which came by at a fast trot . . . .

"Well, you can't anyhow, for you haven't enough school. You can go now, my boy . . ."

Gargantuan crates of appliances and vegetables were moved from the warehouse into truck vans and over to the store. He would sit on the tail-gate of the vehicle, dangling his legs and counting the white markers of the street until his mind spun. And always the hunger gnawing at his growing body. He had coffee with the boys at noon, saving his appetite until night, when he could open a tin of sardines over bread, climaxed by an orange at his lodgings. Wages were low and he was sending half of his pay home to help pay debts on the farm.

Money took on a depressive importance. This was a world of one and five-dollar bills — with them in his possession, he had food, a place to live, and friends. Without it, there was a mysterious and terrible existence which put him in a state of agitation when he dwelled on it. He started to live so close to the skin that one Friday evening he was able to go to the Imperial Bank and open a savings account in which he deposited fifteen dollars and forty cents. The teller who took his money was a middle-aged woman with a heavy fold under her chin. Behind her on a wall hung a painting of a threshing machine in action. He was fascinated by the painting, and stood a long while gazing at it.

The main thoroughfare of the city was a blaze of light at night. He often wandered past the theatre building, taking in display posters of mammoth, virile men and half-clad women, frozen in suggestive poses indicating highlights from the screen drama within. One of the bank buildings had a ticker-tape sign which moved through the same script, informing the observer that saving in this particular bank was in some way connected with vague, overwhelming success. One large billboard outside the Wells of Joy home caught his fancy. It told in bold print that "Jesus *still* saves — On Tuesday at 8:30 pm, Fridays at 7 to 9, and all day Sunday . . . ."

He climbed a high apartment building and found his way to

the roof. Looking down, the city lived and spoke to him in a voice of many tongues. It flashed its million eyes coquettishly, and flirted with its winding streets, where antlike people of the evening moved and babbled the endless poetry of life. And the city laughed up to him, too. Sometimes the laughter was ironic and harsh, coming from the dilapidated rehabilitation home for the crippled, where an outside staircase wound two stories up before reaching the entrance to the clinic. A train roared through an overpass, and an airplane coming in for a landing excited a savage echo from the concrete and the living stone. Far away, the stars of man's making twinkled into the dark meeting of the earth and sky. It was all so magnificent, and it was becoming familiar and close enough to touch, to taste, and to devour and regurgitate into the structures and temples of human industry.

Sleep was an inconstant companion during the long, hot summer. His eyes groped for the ceiling to hang a thought to, but the falling, spiralling night swept about his cheeks and taunted him with restlessness. He drew pictures in the air with a finger he could not see. Lines of poetry tumbled through his mind, but the verses were strange and incomprehensible. He wanted water, but the washroom was a long way down the hall, and the taps pounded through the whole building at night.

He ran a hand over the moist satin of his skin, and his nerves jumped. He touched his genitals, and a flash of fire seared his eyes. Strange and wonderful changes were taking place within his loins, and he panted with excitement at the unaccustomed firmness and size of his protruding organs. His body was in flames, clamoring for another body to lie beside him — against whom he could press and create rhythms of movement until his longings vaporized in one unforgettable, ecstatic moment. Sleep overcame him, and with sleep a startling and beautiful sexual release. He tossed and moaned and pulled his hair with both hands, but the silent walls about him kept their place and their secrets.

Owls screeched in the trees, and the streets were filled with suppressed laughter and the shuffling of passing feet.

•

A chain-smoking, heavy-haired man from the Teamsters Union came into the warehouse to organize the men and boys into his local. There was talk of increased wages and Saturdays off with a five-day week. It was welcome talk, and the response from the workers was immediate.

That afternoon, he was among three who were called into the office to see the personnel manager. He wasn't there, but the general manager faced them with three pay-envelopes in his hand.

"You're fired! Here's your holiday pay and wages . . . and don't let me catch you or your union organizers around here again!"

He walked out into the warm summer day, but the sun was oppressive and the air burnt his throat. He was humiliated and hurt, and events of the past seemed so hopeless suddenly. They got into a car and drove to the Teamsters office, but were told the organizer had left town to visit a construction site. Again the hot sun and scorching wind . . . .

"Let's go get our insurance claim in, mates," said the red-faced Cockney shipper, "our holiday may be a bloody sight longer than our work duration."

. . . Impersonal clerks at the ends of rows marked by sickening yellow paint on a dark, dirty floor. Lines formed a growing crush to the door at the back, with the jobless herded by a stubble-bearded employee of the city police. Scars on the faces and souls of workingmen without work — arrogance, defeat, indifference, childlike incomprehension. His turn came to make his claim, and he fled from his companions to a nearby cafe, where he sat most of the afternoon, drinking coffee and studying the peculiar mauve and yellow checkered decor of the wall across from him.

•

Long weeks of joblessness . . . he slept late and went to bed early to shorten his conscious day. Sometimes he went into the library, but always he was restive and guilty. He took long walks along the river and discovered a community within a community of cave-dwellers — hopeless dregs of humanity who lived, slept, and struggled in old, abandoned coal-mine shafts. He watched them from a distance at first, as they lay stretched out on the ground, or sat up arguing loudly. They cooked food in old tins over open fires, and on bright days they would leave to go foraging in garbage for discarded food and sticks of wood which they brought home for their housekeeping. Once, they motioned to him to come to them, but he shook his head and walked away.

He was frightened and fascinated by them. He met a friend uptown one day, and told him about the junglemen of the city, but the friend was selling insurance and had haughty dreams of success and fortune.

"There you go again — always daydreaming, aren't you? People like that don't exist here or anywhere else, silly. Now you take me — another good year like the last one, and I'll be able to . . ."

He moved out of the hotel into cheaper lodgings. It was a rooming house in the slums of the city, and he occupied a roof garret for ten dollars a month. The room had place for a single, whitewashed bed, a wash-basin, and a tiny desk. He sat on the bed to work at the desk.

Across the hall in the other half of the roof lived two sisters. Jenny was the elder and worked in a garment factory. Minnie was slow-witted, and was employed as a waitress in a five-cents-for-coffee cafe down the street. He often went to this cafe, and when the owner was out, Minnie gave him coffee for nothing. He was growing thin and white. His parents had not been told he was jobless, and he continued sending them money he saved from his unemployment insurance cheques. He saved this money by starving himself.

The sisters overdressed and went out with strange men who

drove fast cars and spoke in overconfident voices. He guessed they were used-car dealers, for their cars changed with each visit. He visited the girls frequently and sat around while they trimmed their fingernails and combed their hair. Their visitors arrived, and one of them turned on him and said, "Isn't the kid a bit young to be hanging around for a piece of tail?" Then the two men laughed, and the girls laughed with them. Humiliation blew in on the wind through the open window, and he returned to his room painfully.

He scanned the want ads for work daily, but there was nothing. He contemplated suicide, and the thought had a sweet, unexplainable assurance. That night he had a violent headache, and he doused his head in cold water again and again in the bathroom downstairs.

Three o'clock in the morning, he put on his light and began writing idly on a piece of paper.

"Each careless bird of summer sings — forever sings . . . ." The pen was poised, but no further words poured out of the ink in the chamber.

The door was flung open forcefully, banging against his leg and waking him. Jenny stood there, frightened and large eyed. Her lipstick was smudged about her mouth and into her cheeks.

"Come on with me. Minnie . . ." she babbled, and pointed down the stairs. Minnie was inside the front door in the small vestibule. She was lying on the floor, and the dim light on the ceiling bloated her face hideously. He bent low over her, and a strange, sweet smell from her mouth turned his stomach. He lifted her and carried her upstairs. She was breathing normally, and her pulse was weak but regular, yet they could not awaken her.

"The guy she was with gave us something to drink in the car. I didn't like it — made me feel kind of hot and funny inside — you know, real crazy like I wanted to take my clothes off. But Minnie, she drank lots of it, and passed out. Her guy was mean . . . slapped her when she did that and called her a pig, and brought us home and left her downstairs . . ." she pursed her lips into the mirror and began cold-creaming her cheeks. His headache returned and he left.

Each pulse was like a hammer-blow against an open wound. Tears burst through the eyelids, and his lips moved in a silent prayer for morning. He was in a half-dream of pain. Doors opened and closed about him, and voices spoke softly through the night, calling his name. A naked thigh moved near his face, and he reached out to touch it, and it stopped moving. His hand explored gently, and a whisper shook the world, trembling his bed, the walls of the sordid room, the pen on his desk, the trousers over the bedrail — the first pale light of dawn . . . and his eyes pierced and steadied the ecstatic tremors of his consciousness.

"I'm dying for a man . . ." The whispered plea became a plaintive wail in the darkest recess of his heart. He rose on his elbow, lifted himself into a sitting position, reached out, and fell into Jenny's arms. She was incredibly soft and warm, and a heady scent rose from her skin to his nostrils. She rippled against him in a panic of urgency. Fiercely, joyously, and with infinite gentleness, he made love for the first time that night. He held her bent in his arms and rocked her, he kissed her and stroked her hair until the iron-scorched ringlets wound about his fingers. Then he pinched her head with his pillow, and as she met his face with moist, slightly opened lips, he told her of his great happiness and deathless devotion to her.

Suddenly, she pushed him aside and left the room. He followed her, but she had latched her door, and he stood in the dusky hallway, naked and confused.

Through his small window, the sun burst into his room, and drab wallpaper walls became golden and liquid. He lifted up his frail arms, and they too became splendid and dressed in the gold of early day. He pulled his covers off and stretched, and felt the surge of new life through his limbs. Then a great weariness overcame him, and he turned his head to one side and slept.

109

His headaches continued throughout the weekend. The other guests of the house left for visits with families and friends, and he was all alone. He took aspirins, but could not eat any food. He left his door open constantly so he could see Jenny when she returned, and he wrote bits of poetry and sketched memories of his childhood.

Late on Sunday night, she returned with her sister. He sprang up and stumbled into the doorway to welcome her. Behind the two sisters were the two men who had given the aphrodisiacs.

She curled her lip at him scornfully and the four of them went into the girls' room. The slamming of their door had a terrible and heartbreaking finality about it, as if the wooden barrier was in some way destined to pronounce joy or doom on all, and the time to utter its judgement had at last come.

Stunned and dazed, he sat on his bed. Hunger and pain welled up through his body, making him tremble violently. Then he put his face into the pillow and cried until his cheeks were bathed in his own tears.

•

On the fringes of civilization, where all the misfits gather, he found employment that winter in a logging camp. It was a dismal season — frosty and with snow to his buttocks. He could never warm his feet, and food and sleep followed each other in a remote and single function each evening.

He shared a cabin with two men. One was bearded and old, and slept with his head raised a few inches from his pillow, held up by a broken and calcified neck which had locked its hold forever. He was too old to work in the woods, and tended the fires of the camp by day. The other man was a young Hercules who worked as a sawyer at the mill. He did pushups and chinned himself from the rafters each morning. At nights he indulged in vigorous and prolonged masturbations.

There was no place to wash or bathe, and the camp was darkened by a brooding and sullen hatred. On payday, all the lights burned late, and there was laughter and singing. Card games sprang up in every cabin, and were followed by fist-fights when winners faced losers after the games. Next day, the human dregs marched off like broken animals into the woods, sullen and silent under a brooding, leaden sky.

He became dulled and lethargic from constant exposure to the frost and snow. At nights, his glare-weary eyes ached, and violent colors flashed before his face, waking him shivering with a sense of loss.

One night, a cabin burned to the ground from an overheated stove. It was a weekend, and two of the occupants had gone into town, leaving behind a third fellow, who was still a boy and had contracted a bad cold. He remembered with horror the police removing the scorched bedstead and springs to which the roasted cadaver was fused by fire. The following day, the mood of the camp was murderous, and it was the first day on which the camp overseer did not visit the woods to scold and urge the men to faster labour. His life wasn't worth the effort, and he had been camp overseer long enough to appreciate the tension and what it signified.

Then one morning the frost on the pines and blackened poplars began falling in large, moist lumps of snow. The clear air seemed deadened, and piercing sounds of sawing and splitting, magnified by the frost, seemed distant and mellow. Somewhere, as through heavy paper, he heard the first bird-call. He had been trimming tree trunks all winter, and his hands became clawlike from the heavy work. He removed his great mittens and studied his hands for the first time, and a strong feeling of pity for his condition cut through his veins, bringing up tears. With profound surprise, he realized this was the first human feeling he had felt all winter. Pity quickly turned to anger, and driving his axe into the wood, he left the work area.

A one-thousand dollar cheque in his shirt pocket . . . and he was riding the lumber-truck back to civilization. Little pools were forming on the road, reflecting a dazzling blue sky. Magpies dove in to scold the intruding vehicle. The driver talked of "chicks" and kept his head bent down listening to an ominous growl in his truck transmission. But the voice and defective machine spoke through billowing warmth and weariness.

On the farm he bathed many times, and his long hair was cut. Then he went to sleep for many days.

He worked the grain cleaner by hand, and saw the snow vanish from the fields. Soon the river ice lifted with hard, breaking sounds and the pulse of the earth struck into full strength and rhythm. The music of stream and bursting greenery infected him, and one afternoon, he packed his things together and walked away up the road. His father was in the barn, and mother in the cellar sorting potatoes when he left. But he spared them sorrow and did not turn back for farewells.

ATHABASCA IMAGES:
AN ESSAY AND TWO FRAGMENTS

SMOKE

As the bluish smoke drifts in with the breezes from some distant forest fire, one's memories go back over the years, for the pungent odour brings back scenes of the days when this northern Alberta of ours was a virgin and untamed land, when men toiled, prayed, hoped and died with the smell of smoke at their nostrils. To the men and women who pioneered this land, the smell of smoke brought inspiration to work harder than ever, for they knew that the day the smoke cleared away, the spirit of the frontier that kept them going would perish, and their ambitions would soon disappear too.

The smoke produced by the burning of clearing piles in the forest is unlike the smoke of cities, which is heavy, musty, nauseating, oily and dark. The smoke of the backwoods is invigorating, faint but unmistakable, and of a bluish tinge. It does not hurt one's eyes as the smoke of cities does.

When the first settlers came to the town of Athabasca some forty years ago, and gazed across the mighty Athabasca River to the dark and formidable forest beyond, they felt disappointed but not in the least disheartened. They had come here to start a new life and to build a new land. Some came to escape oppression in their native lands; such were the Ukrainian immigrants who later arrived from Poland. Some came to cover up and forget a past life and to build anew. Others came to satisfy their craving for more land, and still others came because the urge for new adventure had seized them.

There were some who had plans for returning to their homelands when they first tackled the barren, rugged life of a pioneer. But when they had built a small log cabin and cleared a patch of land and sat on a stump watching the brush piles burning — and smelling the tangy smoke — they made up their minds; they were here and it was here they meant to stay.

There were others who were not as fortunate, or who could not adapt to their new environment. They had no money with which to return to their homelands. They grew to hate the land, the green woods, the fair skies — the settlers' smoke.

For the most part, the settlers were good, earnest, hard-working people who forgot their national differences and petty disputes, and pitched in to help one another build a different, happier and more prosperous life in a new country. These people — Scandinavians, Germans, Poles, Ukrainians, French, and English — loved the smell of smoke.

It was not without hardship and sorrow that the new community began. Many of the pioneers possessed nothing more to start with than the clothes they wore, their two hands, and a group of hungry little mouths to feed. With the aid of the small 'relief' they received from the government, the first thing these people did was to buy some tools and get busy erecting a shelter for themselves and their families. In the small log cabin the cracks were plastered over with mud, while in place of a roof they used a support of logs covered over with dirt. After the shelter was erected, the men and older boys along with the older girls and women of the family each took axe in hand and began hacking away at the dense undergrowth. At the end of a day's work, to go back to the place called home, no matter how crude it was, was heavenly.

"It was hard work, killing hard work," some of the older

people will tell you, "but we were very happy in those days!" Even so, many of the people lost their health and zest for living, long before conditions eased up enough to allow them to enjoy life more or 'take it easy'.

When a patch of ground was cleared and the brush piles burned, the men and boys went to work in some other vicinity as farm hands or common labourers to earn some money to buy an ox or two and a second-hand walking plow. What pride and rejoicing there was when these new possessions were proudly displayed to family and friends for the first time! The next day the difficult task of breaking the heavy, rooted soil began. No one knows how tiresome and patience demanding life can become until he has done plowing with oxen. The big clumsy beasts would lie down, their tongues would hang out and they would stay like that for the rest of the day. Pleading and coaxing made no difference. If the bull felt in a mood for rising, he would, but if not, the exasperated pioneer could only sit down and bemoan his state.

When the plowing was over, there were roots to be gathered, placed in piles and burned. Stones had to be picked off the field and piled before tilling could commence. Occasionally there were huge boulders to be rolled out of the ground and on to stoneboats, on which they were hauled to the stone piles. These boulders cost the health of many a man. The straining and tugging resulted in ruptures and strained muscles. As the men had no time in which to rest and become healed completely, the injuries were never repaired and caused much pain and misery in later life.

When the land was cleared and ready for tilling, the settler found himself with no implements with which to prepare a seed bed. However, they were resourceful. A huge tree was cut down, the branches trimmed and cleaned of twigs so that only stubs about six inches long remained on the trunk. This log was then tied with chains on the two ends and dragged across the field by oxen. This operation, when repeated two or three times, produced reasonably even fields for seeding the grain. Seeding was done by the ancient hand-scattering method. A bag was tied around a man in such a way that it hung within easy arm's reach of the right hand. The bag was then filled with "relief" seed which was scattered over the fields. The seed was covered with earth by dragging a large leafy branch over the field.

When harvesting came on, the sturdy pioneer took his scythe, and calling his womenfolk out to bind the cut grain into sheaves, went to work. Threshing was done by the old-fashioned flail. The sheaved grain was placed on a hard floor where it was beaten. The straw was then thrown aside, leaving the separated chaff and kernels. On a windy day, the chaff and kernels were dropped through the air; the chaff was carried away and the clean, plump kernels remained. The harvest could not be sold, but was kept as seed for next year's crop. Winters were spent in making and selling or bartering railroad ties for flour and sugar and other necessities. Too often the men spent the winter in the bush in inadequate clothing.

Thus the life of the builders of Northern Alberta went on from year to year. When they had gained a few possessions, meagre perhaps, such as a cow or horse or a few pigs, the great depression of the 1930s struck. What a set-back it was for these people to lose their small belongings to pay pressing debts! However, this was just one of the many disappointments that they encountered in their struggle for a living. They took it all with resolution and determination. Through the years, they had learned the virtue of patience — these people who loved the singing of the birds, the green forests, no matter how hard they struggled against them, the sunny skies of Alberta, the vastness of the land, the new liberty that they enjoyed here, and the bitter-sweet smell of the smoke that called them back to the land from which these hardy folk had sprung.

There was a finer side in the lives of these pioneer people.

The seclusion of the life they led brought the family close together. There was a mutual feeling that does not prevail in any other place in as large a degree as in a lone log cabin in the wild.

The settlers soon realized that the hard life they led did nothing to spread culture and civilization among the growing children. In 1929 they started the first school in the community and in the early '30s they put up a small log building that, though it has been replaced by a more modern building, stands to this day. In 1933, a community hall was erected, a large log structure that was unbearably cold during the winter months. Here the younger people held dances, dramatic concerts, singing practices, and motion pictures. Here, also, on Sundays, the children were taught the language and culture of the old lands from which their parents had come. There are few young people who cannot read and write the languages of their parents' native lands. The elders, too, began to take a more active interest in the cultural life of the new land and in the affairs of the nation. They joined societies in the community and they formed various political associations. There was a general rush for naturalization papers. They wanted to become real Canadian citizens, to exercise their right to vote and thus have a direct say in the government.

When the Depression years were over, the elderly and tired pioneers, the ''firsts'' in the district, encouraged the younger generation to join organizations for the betterment of the farmer. They wanted no repetition of the Hungry Thirties which had affected them so drastically.

The settlers' lot was improving; tractors and cars were owned by the majority; each had many acres of land to work; farming methods were improving, and as a result crop yields were higher; the price of grain was rising; everything pointed for the better — when the war broke out in 1939. The younger generation had watched with growing chagrin as the fascist cloud spread over Europe, for though they were Canadians by birth, there was still European blood flowing in their veins. Everyone realized that Canada was endangered. The young people who, because of the pure life they had led, had grown into strong men and women, strong in spirit, body and mind, dropped what they were doing and enlisted in the armed forces. The older, weary pioneers took up the work they had started some twenty, thirty, or forty years ago, with renewed vigor and determination. Everyone went "all out" to help the war effort. They would never allow the Nazis to destroy their new-found and hard-earned liberty.

In the muddy trenches on the European battlefields, amid the sulphuric smells of gunpowder, these Albertans recalled the scent of another smoke they had smelled so often. To them this was a symbol of the pioneer's spirit in which they had been reared and which they fought so desperately to preserve now. Hitler wasn't going to get Canada if they could help it!

Today, everything is peaceful and serene in this community; it is a thriving farm district like so many others in northern Alberta. Yet it is different — for when a dry spell of spring weather arrives, and there is a faint whiff of pungent, bitter-sweet bush fire smoke on the air, an old man will pick up an axe from the woodshed and make off for the few remaining acres of bush or forest left on the farm.

The pioneer blood in him has been stirred.

THE PITCHFORK

"Silly bugger," said the old man after much deliberation as he leaned against the tree in his meadow, a pitchfork imbedded in his back. He rolled a cigarette with the pitchfork in him, lit it, and smoked it to the shortest possible butt before spitting it out and snuffing it under his cracked gray leather boot.

He had hired me as a boy labourer at wages of five dollars a day. The day beginning at dawn and ending in darkness. He grew wild hay in a sour hayfield and sold it in late winter when the price was highest to farmers who kept dairy cattle and were faced with feed shortages. The hay was lush and rank, yet curing in the sun I remember always how sweet and lemony it smelled.

When I met him in the field at first light of dawn, he was already there, his wagon rick half-loaded, his horses droop headed, their tails swishing away mosquitoes and horse flies, which droned incessantly in the still northern summer air.

"You sleep in? Your mother forgot to wake you? You got to learn to get up on time, you know," he chided me with a half-smile on his lips, his ancient blue eyes clear and penetrating. It was uncomfortable to be stared at by him. I couldn't find the words to lie, apologize, or explain. Each truth as I knew it then would seem to have a deception he would

121

immediately examine unmercifully. So I grinned and said nothing. He nodded, appearing to take this as a surrender worthy of his great age and community importance as provisioner of sour hay when it mattered. And we began the work of collecting and moving the hay from the meadow to the storage stacks he maintained in the front yard of his farmhouse.

Every morning at hay-harvest time was like another. The coolness of night evaporated once the sun rose over surrounding dark forests of tamarack and poplar and illuminated the clearings, which had been cultivated into barley fields, pastures, and locations for construction of farm buildings. The heat of late summer quickly became intense, the flies and mosquitoes alarming in their numbers and persistence for animal blood. The horses were now restive and irritated. They snorted, tossed their heads to clear pests from around their noses and eyes. If this failed, they sometimes bolted for a short distance, pursued by the two of us. But the attempt at running away was never serious, and a few shouted commands from the old man usually brought them to a standstill.

We loaded hay with pitchforks from both sides of the wagon. Some of the slipery hay on my side slid off the load, and the old man calmly helped me reload as he explained what I had done wrong.

"A lick of hay on the edge of the load requires another in the middle so's each dovetails the other and holds the load together. Understand that, an' I'll pay you six dollars a day."

Even though I thought I understood and made this correction early in working with him, he never did increase my wages above five dollars a day. Which pleased me, because I considered it the only flaw I could find in his character. Until I discoverd another one.

"Never, but never climb up a loaded hay wagon with your pitchfork in your hands," he scolded me when I did just that. "If you should miss a handhold an' fall, the fork's in your hands. You can fall on it an' drive it through your guts. Or it might fall on top of you an' hurt your head or face."

"How would you do it proper?" I asked, knowing he would tell me anyway. He smiled, then raising his own pitchfork like a spear to his shoulder, he stepped back from the wagon.

"You throw it upward, tines first, to the sky. As it sails over your load of hay, you'll throw it in such a way as to make the tines arc downward. It falls on the hayload an' penetrates into the hay an' remains there as if you'd forced it in by hand while standing on top of the load, which you ain't. I've put my pitchfork in that way an' driven seven miles without correcting it. When I arrived where I was going, it was still in place, as it should've been."

Saying this, he drew a deep breath and exhaled with a whoosh as he threw the gleaming implement upward toward the top of the load of hay. The pitchfork sailed smoothly in a gentle arc, the polished tines gleaming in a flickering reflection of the sun. Then it tilted downward toward the wagon, but he had thrown it too far to the front. With a pinging sound one of the tines struck the wooden edge of the wagon load frame. Deflecting upward and back toward us came the pitchfork. The old man blinked once as he stared at it, then turned and stumbled away in a clumsy, arthritic gait.

"Run!" he hollered. "The goddamned thing's comin' back!"

I didn't run. I moved quickly into the shadow and shelter of the wagon rick. The flying fork pursued the old man. He stumbled for the shelter of the nearby poplar tree. His logic was confused, as was his retreat — his long white hair bobbing from under the edges of his straw hat, his arms out, his legs wobbling as he hurried away. The fork was completing its return arc now, coming down to the left of the old man, tines spearing toward the ground. At the last possible moment the old man hesitated and turned sharply to the left. The tines of the fork came into his back at a sharp angle, stabbing through his jacket, shirt and skin.

"Hah!" he exclaimed with pain and surprise. He stood still

for a moment, the fork in his lower back quivering in time to his breathing. He then slowly moved to the tree he had been trying to reach and leaned against it with his shoulder. Carefully, he withdrew his leather tobacco pouch.

"Silly bugger," he said. Then he smoked, and after snuffing out the remnant of his cigarette under his boot, he turned and knelt in front of the tree. Reaching out to take hold of the poplar trunk with both his hands, he ordered me to pull the pitchfork out of his back. I did, bracing my foot against his hard, shriveled shoulder. I was surprised at how easily the sharp implement could be extracted from the old man's body. I pulled and it slipped out with no more difficulty than pulling it out of soft clay . . . .

ONE OCTOBER EVENING

One October evening, alone on a country road leading to the mountainous country, she died. Alone, with startling suddeness, her last cry echoing and fading through snow dusted trees, the rattle of roadside gravel under the wheels muted by the howl of the motor of the dented old car racing towards the mountains — towards oblivion.

"Fuckin' breed whore!" Rosa heard the man with his head out the car window shout almost at the moment of impact. She had been walking to exercise away a numbing headache which had persisted for most of her work day at the bank. After dinner she had retired to her room in the Stoney Creek Hotel. She tried to rest, but the cattlemen were in town for a convention. They idled their trucks and shouted to each other above the motor noises from the street below her window. It was a cheerful, busy sound. But it kept her from sleeping. So she rose and wrote a letter to her mother. The letter was short, apologizing for not having written sooner and explaining how, on graduation from business school, she had found employment with the Bank of Commerce. She then briefly explained her desire to see the interior of the country, and how she had applied for, and been given a transfer to this northern town. She was about to elaborate on the shortage of housing she found here, and how for two weeks now her home was a hotel room, but her thoughts were interrupted by a commotion outside the hotel.

She rose and pushed the curtains aside at her window. In the street below two men were arguing with a woman beside an older car which was parked in the street, its motor running. The men were dressed in heavy padded coats with parkas. The coats were open, the men agitated. They looked dark, large and menacing against the pale, snow-covered street. As Rosa watched, one of the men pulled money out of his pocket and offered it to the woman, who refused to accept it. The man then roughly took hold of her and pushed the money down the neck of her blouse. The woman laughed and the man slapped her. She began running away and the man moved to follow her. But his companion restrained him and they both returned to the car. A third man, driving the car, moved the vehicle forward with a lurch and followed the woman fleeing on foot down the sidewalk. Through the open windows of the car, the men shouted obscenities at her.

Rosa shuddered and closed the curtains of her window. She addressed and sealed the letter to her mother, gathered her coat, and went downstairs, having decided she needed a walk to exercise away her headache and to lift a sense of unease which the incident she had witnessed had left her with.

The night air was cold and crisp, the snow under her feet squeaked with an unfamiliar sound as she moved through the small knots of men huddled in doorways and beside ranch vehicles smelling acidly of manure and fuel oil. They were shy men, nervous in town. But to her they were unfamiliar and she avoided brushing against them as she walked past the hotel towards the brightly lit main street of the town.

"If the price drops again, I'm scrubbin' my breedin' stock . . . "

"You're lucky. I can't even do that. Owe too much . . . gotta keep goin' as best I can . . ."

It was bits of desolate conversation she overheard. The information meant little to her, for she was a stranger to this town. She knew ranch people — had grown up among them as a child. But they had been carefree men and women of the sun, sharing difficult lives and rejoicing in small advantages. These people, among whom she now found herself, were different. They were cold and sullen, much as the dark forests and snow-covered hills were chill and forbidding. They spoke and argued over the sounds of machines which they seemed incapable of turning off, and whose acrid fumes and steam they appeared indifferent to. Well behaved in shops and public buildings, they were capable of sudden and unpredictable violence in the streets and in private dwellings.

In her growing apprehension, Rosa walked faster. She was suddenly startled to realize she had walked away from the lights of the town. Her walk had taken her out alone into the country on [manuscript ends here]

ATHABASCA STORIES:
SELECTIONS FROM "POOR PEOPLE"

LOVE BY PARCEL POST

"A man's got to have a woman — same's a motor's got to have a spark plug!" Bill Welensky said, sucking his cheeks into his toothless mouth, and taking another swig from the bottle of beer I had given him.

"Sure, sure, Bill. But spark plugs are out of style with you. A motor your age should be retired. How old are you anyway?" I asked with some annoyance. I hadn't believed this nonsense when I first heard of it. So when old Bill came visiting my place, I asked him right off — and old Bill didn't mince any words replying. I was hoping he'd deny all the rumours, but now that he didn't, I got sore.

"Seventy-three!" He said defiantly. "Anyway, what difference does it make? You're forty, and just look at you — guts hanging out — shoulders sloping. Me? I'm in better shape than you are any day. It isn't age makes a man rundown. Look!"

He put down his bottle and rose from his chair. Quickly, he unbuttoned his shirt, and then puffing out his chest he flexed his arms back. He was in good shape all right. White-haired and parched as he was, he still had a sound body.

"See!"

"Sure — I can see, Bill. Still . . . at your age . . ."

131

Bill had a son as old as me. Paul was his name. Got married and took up a farm over the ravine. Grew potatoes for the green market in town, and made a passable living at it. But he worked like a horse to make ends meet — all the Welenskys worked like horses ever since I knew them. Even the old mother, whom they buried eighteen years ago when she died of exhaustion trying to pull a calf out of a starving cow at birth. The cow and the woman died, but the calf lived. Old Bill gave the calf his wife's name — Martha. The critter is still around — even bears some resemblance to the woman. Same slow walk and piles of skin hanging under her chin.

It had been Paul who first told me of old Bill's intentions.

"You know what the old devil's up to, Sid? He's getting himself a wife by mail order! A young thing, too — from one of those refugee camps in Germany. Jesus! You should see the picture she sent him. Just a kid — no more than twenty, twenty-five!"

"What?"

The news had been hard to take. Here was me — forty years of age, with a clear title to a hundred and sixty acres of land — ten head of cattle — a fifty-five model Chev all paid for, and a two-room house — and what chance did I have of getting a wife? Sure, there were plenty of girls to be driven to dances or into town — but try to push a notion of marriage into their heads, and they'd just pass a guy on to another of their friends. Bet I've spent ten dollars a week on gasoline, oil and tires in the last five years trying to get married.

Old Bill swallowed the last of his beer and threw the bottle over the porch rail into the grass alongside my house. I had half a mind to make him go and pick it up. Every character who ever stops at my house for a beer and chin-wag throws his empties habitually over the railing in the same place. This summer I'll try cutting the grass to see if it will make any difference.

"All right," I said. "Let's see the photograph!"

Old Bill was blank as a wall when he looked at me.

"What photograph?"

"You know what I'm talking about! Show me the photograph of this parcel-post woman of yours. Paul said you had one, so let's see her!"

Bill sort of yawned and stretched, but I could see him tighten up to make a run for it. Before he could rise from his chair, I was over him with my fist knotted in front of his nose.

"I'll paste you one!" I threatened. "I'm not running a tavern here for old lovers — now let's see her!"

Bill knew I meant business and reluctantly he pulled out his frayed wallet. Painfully, he thumbed through cream cheque stubs, bits of waxed string, and five-year old tax assessments. Under all this mess was this coloured photograph.

"Good God!" I exclaimed.

Paul hadn't lied. The woman in the picture couldn't have been more than twenty. Yellow haired she was, with city-made curls right down her neck. Eyes as blue as the sky, and lips full and rich like Sonia Harrison used to have before she married the dentist — the one who turned queer on her.

"Pretty good, eh?" Old Bill was proud as a rooster, and he gave himself the liberty of another luxurious yawn. I shoved the coloured picture back in his hand.

"Get out of here before I kick you clear across the road!" I snapped, and he shrugged his shoulders and left.

I had a fair amount of summer fallowing to do the next two weeks. This far north, you've got to get your summer fallow cultivated in season, or the weeds come up thick as a carpet — so I didn't have much chance to get out or hear any country-side news.

Then one Friday morning just as I was beginning to grease my tractor for the day's work, old Bill came calling again. He had a white shirt on and a faded blue tie. Bill always wore heavy winter trousers, but now he wore a pair of light brown pants, washed and pressed, after a fashion, by hand. Over his arm he carried a leather windbreaker. His grey canvas running shoes had most of the grease rubbed off them. I looked up from under the tractor where I was working, and saw he'd even vaselined his white hair down and combed it back.

"Where's your cap, Bill? You gonna catch an earache like that!"

He rubbed his gnarled hand with embarrassment over his chin, and this sort of put him off, for he'd shaved and the skin was more or less smooth to the touch. He shuffled his feet a lot, which brought dust into my face.

"Cut it out!" I shouted. "You'll get dirt in the bearings!"

"Oh — to hell with your bearings!"

Old Bill suddenly came down on his haunches so he could see me.

"Come out and drive me into town. I'll pay you good." He said in a rapid, breathless voice.

I crawled out.

"Jesus, Bill — what's eating you? You look like a . . . ," I began.

"Never mind that!" He got snappy. "Just drive me into town."

"I don't understand." I said. And then I *did* understand, and I roared with laughter.

"I see — she's arriving for the slaughter! Boy! This I got to see!"

Bill squirmed and a pleading sort of look came into his eyes, so I didn't push him any more.

"All right," I said. "Let me change my clothes and I'll take you in."

As we were walking to the house, I thought of something.

"Say! Does Paul know she's coming? We better pick up Paul so she can meet your family at the station."

"No!" Bill jumped like he'd been hit. "No need of that! There's time for things like that later!"

"I see — you didn't tell her you been married before! You're gonna surprise her a little at a time!'' I said sarcastically. Bill clammed up.

We reached town a half-hour before the train, and old Bill did a powerful lot of smoking. He had ashes all over the front seat of my car, and butts smoldering all around under his feet. I could have gotten after him to keep tidier, but he was sweating a lot with nervousness and there was no point in bugging him.

"Bill," I said after awhile. "How much this adventure going to cost you? The way I see it, you're not going anyplace — she's coming here. And I don't figure she's fool enough to think she's getting a prize — so you're paying in some way."

"It's already cost," Bill said gruffly. "One-way ship fare an' two hundred in cash!"

"That's about five hundred dollars! You could of bought a car for that money, or set it aside and guaranteed yourself a proper burial, Bill . . ."

Old Bill winced.

"Suppose she don't come, Bill? Suppose she takes your money and hightails it into Paris, or some other fast-living place? She's a young and pretty girl, Bill. Suppose she even takes your money so she can afford to marry someone over there?"

Bill squirmed and fired up another cigarette. The cloud of smoke he blew made it impossible to see the station platform through the windshield of my car. I stuck my hand out and felt for wind direction, then turned the car so we got a cross-draft across the front seat.

"She ain't gonna trick me — I'd put her in jail if she did!" Bill threatened darkly when some of the smoke had cleared.

I shrugged my shoulders and said no more. Then we heard the train whistle, and it was like a pin in the backside for Bill. He almost hit the car roof with his head. In a moment, the train appeared, coming to a grinding stop at the station. The stationmaster and his boy materialized out of nowhere and began unloading parcels and mail.

"Could be she's in one of those packages," I teased. "Watch for one with a ribbon around it!"

Bill was out of the car and galloping for the platform. I followed, and noticed he had withdrawn her photograph and was holding it in his hand. But the platform was empty — and there was no indication any passengers would leave the train, even though the step had been lowered on the coach car.

"Sid! What we gonna do?" Bill turned on me, and there was panic in his eyes. "Maybe like you said . . . but hell! The letter promised . . . Oh, think of something, Sid!"

I really wanted to help him at that moment. But I could think of nothing, so I walked away from him toward the shady side of the station building, where I leaned against the wall and lit up a smoke.

I saw her first — the fat lady with pillarlike ankles and a heavy felt coat. She struggled wearily out of the train, holding a paper bag in one hand, and a large hat in the other. She seemed frightened, and hesitated to step down on the platform. But the conductor back of her gave her a gentle shove, and pulled up the step behind her immediately.

Then the train began inching away.

She looked up and down the railway platform, and seeing me, came slowly forward.

"Meester Beel Welensky . . ." she said when she was within speaking distance. I shut my eyes so tight I saw white lines cross my eyeballs.

"Isabella!"

It was a kind of wild shout Bill gave just then. Now I opened my eyes, and saw them standing a yard away from one another, both wilted with uncertainty and shame. Bill was the first to move forward, holding up the photograph in his hand.

"This picture . . ." He began.

"My daughter . . . She ees so happy in Berlin . . ." The woman suddenly dropped her things and began to cry. Bill hesitated a moment, then throwing his shoulders back, he walked boldly

136

towards her. He took her arm and gently urged her toward my car. I picked up her belongings and followed.

"Where to?" I asked when I started up the car motor.

"Take us to Paul's! I'll pay you good!" Old Bill said in a firm voice. He turned his face to the woman.

"You know my Paul, Isabella! Paul is my son. The photograph you have is my son, Paul!"

Bill spoke slowly, deliberately, so she would understand every word. She understood, for I heard her sob.

We were on the road and headed back for the farm when Bill nudged me with his elbow. I turned and he looked me right in the eye and winked.

"You got a new suit to wear as best man, Sid?" He asked slyly.

I looked past him. Isabella was watching him and me — and she was smiling.

THE MEEK SHALL INHERIT

I am a forgotten, unknown citizen of my country. A statistic lost among others. But maybe some clerk noticed my name in the endless record of marriages sifting through his hands — and maybe his pencil stopped alongside my name and made a mark there, while he had himself a dirty laugh.

I can hear him, like I hear so many other sounds now. He is saying to the men around him, "Hey, lookit this! Some broad named Brenda Tyson, aged sixteen, married Tom Beckitt, aged seventy-six — out there in gravel country. Boy, the old guy must be rich or just lucky!"

And they all have a good laugh. Then more names, more stories pile up on their desks, and I am forgotten even as a statistic.

I don't wish to be forgotten. I want to cry out loud so they can hear me beyond the river and hills. I want to stand square before Parson Claye, look right into his eyes so he can't get away from me, and tell him how he lied and what a terrible crime he committed against me. I want to take down the Winchester my father left me, which is gathering dust in the attic — to load it up and go after my husband.

I want him to look up from his work in the fields. I want to see fear in his goat eyes — and then I want to shoot him dead. Keep shooting until he stops grunting — I want to be sure he'll never get up anymore. Then I want to run down the road to find my peg-leg man who was kind to me once.

Parson Claye was over to my house yesterday. There are only eight families left on the gravel flats, so if anyone misses church on Sunday, he always comes calling the next day to ask the reason.

"Brenda," he spoke in that strong voice which has terrified me from childhood. "I was going past, and thought I'd call."

"It's good of you." I looked over my shoulder, avoiding his fierce gaze, for it was an accusing, burning stare he always gave me and I had to avert my eyes for fear he would stop my breath.

"Where's Tom?"

I nodded towards the field, where my husband was weeding a long row of potatoes.

"What happened yesterday?" I knew he would ask, and I had an answer ready, but now I could not speak.

"I dunno." I shrugged my shoulders, and suddenly felt my face break out in perspiration. Another opportunity came and went. This was my chance to tell him — explain how frightened I was — how ashamed and hot I became in the presence of my neighbours. Already I could hear the boys snickering behind my back, pointing their fingers in my direction and making obscene signs with their hands. The men, watching the flesh of my neck, and the women smiling wisely to themselves. Our church was not a house of worship — it was a court — a forum where the guilty came time and again to be tried and punished for a crime no one could remember anymore.

Armed with the Word of the Lord, Parson Claye was judge and jury over me. It was so on the day my father died, and it has been so ever since.

The day my father was nearing his end, he sent me to fetch the parson. I was sixteen then. I'd never been to school, for the nearest schoolhouse was sixteen miles distant, and our land was too poor to afford me leaving it. I had to work from daylight to night keeping us alive. There was nobody to play with, for our people were leaving farms for jobs in Great Falls when the drought came. The fathers and mothers and their children left. Those who stayed behind were the sick, like my own father, and those who were afraid because they were aging and could never be hired for work.

I brought the parson to Father's bedside. The light of the setting sun came through the dirty window, throwing deep shadows over Father's face. Where the sun touched his cheekbones and forehead, the skin seemed to melt, like wax under heat. I had to look away, for death was in the room now, crowding and choking me.

"Take care of Brenda," Father whispered hoarsely. "See she marries and lives well."

Parson Claye nodded and gave his word, and Father lay back, closing his eyes forever.

I brought in the crop that autumn, and when I had the potatoes piled into pits and covered with earth, and the corn in the threshing shed, Parson Claye came to see me with Tom Beckitt riding a horse behind him.

Old man Beckitt lived on the far end of the gravel flats. In the past we hadn't mixed with him much, and this was the first close look I had of him.

He looked like a goat, with grey tufts of hair growing out of his ears, little fleshy eyes, and a straggly, yellowed beard. When he dismounted from his horse and came towards me, he even smelled like a goat. I started to laugh, and Parson Claye looked hard at me.

"What for you laughing, Brenda?" he demanded sharply.

"Him!" I pointed to Beckitt, for in those days I was young, and said what I thought.

Parson Claye took my arm in an iron grip and pulled me forward.

"Don't you ever laugh at him again!" he roared. He let me

go then, and looking down at his feet said, "Tom Beckitt wants to marry you."

I looked at the old man, who was grinning at me with a mouth of missing and decayed teeth. I giggled nervously.

The parson was still fidgeting with his feet, avoiding looking at me.

"You can't do better, Brenda. There's no men your age about anymore. I promised your father to see you married and done well by. Tom is a good man."

I tried to fight back the tears, but they came like a bucket turned over inside my head.

"Look at it this way, child!" The parson sounded both angry and sorry now. "Tom is seventy-six — he can't live too much longer. Give him a few years of happiness, and in turn he will leave his farm to you. There will be no suffering — it is not too much to ask."

"No!" I shouted. "Go away — I have a place to live on!"

"You don't know what you're saying!" The parson took a step towards me, and I quickly moved away. I began to cry again. I must have cried away the afternoon, for when I looked up, the sky was deepening with evening, and both the parson and Tom Beckitt were gone.

A community like ours, where living is hand to mouth, is hard and cold to itself and to others. Father used to have neighbours and friends call in to see him when he was ill. But now, a great loneliness fell over the farm. No one stopped to visit — no one even turned to look into the yard when the odd wagon rumbled by on the way to town or back. There were moments when I panicked, and stood by the roadside for hours, staring up and down the hot trail of dust for the sight of a human. At nights, I would often sit in a dark corner of the house, shivering in the autumn winds which came down from the mountains, wet and cold.

Then came the night when I could stand it no more. All that day, I could not eat. My cheeks burned as if with fever, and

141

my tongue felt thick and spongy. I lit the lamp when darkness fell, and made a pot of tea, which I could not drink. Exhausted and sick, I sat in a chair to rest. I must have fallen asleep immediately.

In sleep, my mind played games with me. I heard a terrible roar, and over it the booming voice of Parson Claye proclaiming as he did in church on Sundays — "Suffer but a while longer, brethren — for the meek shall inherit the world!"

Then I saw him, crossing the fields of the gravel flats, with flames bursting in his footsteps. He seemed to be making his way across the land towards me. I felt the heat he made in his approach. It burned my cheeks, and as I stepped back, I felt the walls of my house behind me go up in flames. I tore at my clothes, for my skin was at the point of igniting. Then I turned and ran.

"It is the wrath of the Lord." I heard myself gasp. "He is coming to destroy me, for I have disobeyed!"

I rounded the house and was about to break away into the open fields beyond, when suddenly Tom Beckitt rose out of the earth to bar my way. But now he was no longer the man — he had become an upright goat, with horns growing from his crinkly brow, and his cloven feet pawing obscenely at the ground.

I screamed, and threw myself down to the ground in fear and shame.

Then I woke. The lamp in my kitchen was still burning and the room had turned cold. My face was moist, and I could not stop the trembling of my body.

That night, I went to Tom Beckitt, bruising my feet on the pebbles in the fields as I ran to his farm. Many times I fell in the darkness, but I did not stop to rest, for the night was hostile and I was afraid.

The next Sunday we were married. As Parson Claye gave his blessings to the old man and myself, he smiled. I had never seen him smile before, and it relieved the heavy burden on my heart. I was about to smile back, when he spoke to Tom.

"There may be no children of this union, but there will be happiness, for Brenda is a girl of spirit, and strong!" He winked secretively at Tom. A woman in the pew behind us heard, and giggled. My mouth turned dry, and I bent my head with shame. Once again, I was alone and frightened. I wanted to run out of the church — all the way to where my father was buried. To lean my ear against his grave and listen for some friendly, comforting word. Instead, I remained at old Tom Beckitt's side, staring in confusion at the floor which was alive with ants and sand beetles.

I hated the smell and touch of my husband. At nights, I insisted he leave the bedside lamp lit, but this did little to cool his ardour. So in despair and to give our marriage the sordid, detached relationship which I felt, I made him leave two dollars each time he lay with me. In the mornings, when he rose early and went out to work, I would gaze at the money, feeding my shame and unhappiness with the sight of it.

Spring came after a long and cold winter. Tom was behind with his work of cleaning seed and repairing machinery, so I saw little of him for days on end. I did nothing to help him — he even had to make his own meals. I wanted him to get tired of me, to order me away and thereby give me back the freedom I craved so much. But he said nothing. It was as if this was the life he expected with me. Which made me all the more frantic.

One day, I walked further away from home than was my habit. On the last bluff overlooking the river, I saw smoke from a small fire. I made my way towards it, and saw a man heating coffee in a tin can. He saw me approaching, and raised himself painfully to greet me. On one of his legs, the trouser was cut away to reveal a wooden peg from the knee down.

"Hello!" I shouted, and despite myself, hurried towards him. He lifted his hand and grinned.

I had never seen him before, and yet I knew him. I knew

the pain in his heavy eyes, the hungry cheek and slow, nodding movements of a man born to be a stranger to pleasure. It was the face of my own father at a time when I was not yet conceived.

We said nothing. We only watched one another, eating out in silence the experiences each of us had lived through. Then we drank his coffee — passing the can back and forth, he drinking from the side my lips had touched, and me drinking from where he had drunk.

A cloud passed over the sun, and we lay side by side in the dead winter grass. I did not rise in the evening, but turned my hot cheek to the earth and watched him hobble away from me, following the gravel bluff until he became a speck on the horizon. Then he vanished altogether.

Tom Beckitt came and found me. I looked him straight in the face as I rose and buttoned up my clothes. He fumbled with his thin, aged hands, then turned away from me.

"Come home," he said in a tired, piping voice. "You're still my wife."

Tom Beckitt never spoke to me again, but he must have talked to Parson Claye, and the parson must have gossiped to the neighbours, for the women turn up their heads and sniff the air when I pass, and men stop talking and crowd around me. And I can find no pride — no courage to stand erect and speak what I think.

Once I thought the hour of comfort would sustain me forever. But when the peg-leg man vanished over the hills, my thirst for life first turned into a sad longing, and then into a devouring lust which I took great pains to contain for fear it would destroy me.

Among my belongings which I moved to Tom Beckitt's house is my father's Winchester rifle. It hangs in the attic, gathering dust. I go up often to stare at it, to wrap my thoughts, plans, and dreams around its blue steel and faded wooden stock.

On Sundays, when I go to church, Parson Claye directs his sermons at me — throwing furious words at me like barbs.

"Repent! Repent before the Lord, you who are soiled — for you must be meek to meet your Saviour!" he thundered at me the last meeting I went to. I hung my head, felt the gazes of the wayward men burn my bare neck, felt Tom stir uncomfortably beside me and smelled the musk of his sweat. I thought of the rifle, I thought of the evil influence of the parson — I thought of my dirty marriage and I thought of my father and the peg-leg man. Yet I couldn't lift my head and do what I had to do — couldn't cool the red heat of my cheeks which marked me with the stamp of the slut.

But I will — so help me, Lord! I will! I must lift up my head and strike out. It is late already, and the young life is struggling, demanding from my womb that I shed the burden of these gravel flats. Tomorrow I will act.

Tomorrow I will follow my peg-leg man!

GOLD IN THE ASPENS

When the sun is setting low, the day's work done, and all talk that must be spoken has been spoken — our folks take a few moments to sit on their porches, sort of looking through one another at nothing and thinking sad evening thoughts. And it is at a time like this that someone remembers and tells the story of Elmer McGee and Polly.

The story is told quietly, and never in the presence of complete strangers, for our memories are secrets which only the blue hills and aspen-covered valleys share. I have heard the story of Elmer and Polly many times in the years I have lived here, but we never tire of hearing or telling it again. For our stories are as old and intimate as prayers to us.

Someone — his name escapes me now — once made up a song around the story. It has been sung up and down this valley by good singers, young and old. Even I have sung it a few times, chording along on my six-dollar guitar:

> Come listen I'll tell you the sad bitter tale,
> Of old Jonas Barton, who is dying in jail . . .
> Of a handsome young fellow named Elmer McGee
> Who died for the love of poor wretched Polly . . . .

When he took Polly for his wife, Jonas Barton was an old man, stooped, with long gray whiskers curled down the sides of his thin face. He had the cold, pale eyes of a parson, and he walked slowly, burdened with the hardships of endless years.

Polly was young — a mere girl then. She came from across the next range of hills, which you can just see from the porch of my house. Thin as a blade of grass, she had large pale blue eyes which looked at you like those of a wondering child. Her bare feet and face were tanned by the sun until they seemed brown as the earth after the passing of a light summer rain. The farm Jonas and Polly lived on is over there — just across the valley. If you look where I'm pointing you can just make out where their white stone house still stands.

Elmer lived on this side of the valley, over to the right. There were three in his family — Elmer, his older brother, Jack — and their mother. Elmer's father had been dragged to death by a couple of runaway horses when Elmer was still too young to walk.

As you can see, between the two farms, then as now, lies our valley — overgrown with thick aspens which folks cut down for firewood each autumn. The valley has always remained government property, as nobody has need of it for farmland. So it has always been used as common pasture for cattle.

Each evening, it falls upon the youngest in each family to go into the valley, to find and bring the cattle home for milking. And so it was that early in the first summer Polly came to live among us, Elmer and she met among the aspens while searching for their cattle.

Elmer is remembered as a fine cut of a boy — dark haired and tall as a man, even at fifteen — with the strong mouth, and dark, laughing eyes of his father. One summer day gave way to another. And as the days passed, Elmer left for the valley of aspens earlier and returned home with the cattle later.

Then one night, Jack woke from a troubled sleep, and found his brother's bed empty and undisturbed. Jack has told of how he rose and went to the window. He has told of looking out

147

the window into the yard, white and liquid with moonlight — and seeing Elmer naked at the well, washing himself lovingly — his body white as beautiful granite there in the moonlight.

The weeks galloped by now, and when the time of gold in the aspens came, Polly was growing large with child. Jonas Barton was the last man to notice, for he was an old man, and he and Polly were strangers to each other.

"Who is your lover?" He demanded one day, trembling as with cold when he spoke. Polly turned her face to the wall, but would not reply.

He asked again, this time his voice trembling, but still she was silent. Jonas rose to his feet, and pointing an accusing finger at her, spoke in a voice thin with jealousy.

"You will tell me who he is, or leave my house forever, to become a beggar on the road for your wickedness!"

Like the child she was, Polly became terrified at this threat of banishment. Without turning her face to him, she babbled to her husband about Elmer McGee and how she met him at milking times, and in the nights when the valley was asleep.

There was mist in the hills the next morning — a pale mist like thin smoke which lingers after a fire. On this morning, Jonas rose early, took his old rifle from the wall and left his home, while Polly slept. And as Polly slept, Jonas crossed this valley, stopping only when he reached the well before the house where Elmer McGee lived.

"Elmer McGee — come out! I am waiting for you!"

The old man called loudly, his dew-wet clothes clinging to his thin body as to a field scarecrow.

Elmer rose from his bed and walked to the window, through which he saw and heard the old man. He bowed his head and stepped outdoors into the misty morning.

He was a brave boy — a good boy!

Jack said he walked out and stood facing the old man, but he neither pleaded for his life nor turned to run away. When the rifle shot thundered through the valley and spent itself against those hills, Elmer McGee fell to the ground, the red blood spurting high from his chest.

They came in a big car and took Jonas Barton away. Some say Jonas Barton will hang one day, and some say he will not, but will forever remain in prison. And some have said Jonas Barton died long ago of a broken heart. But news comes slowly and through many mouths into our hills.

Our people buried Elmer McGee on the hillside facing the sun, as we have buried our kind for generations. Polly was alone now, and her fields turned golden, then white without harvest. Daily she came to the place where Elmer lay buried, and the sun and wind dried the tears into salty ashes on her cheeks.

Then one afternoon, Jack went to sit at Elmer's graveside, and he met Polly there — thin and dark in face and her body swelled to bursting. Without saying a word, he took her arm and led her to her home, following this very road. He made her sit on the bench in front of Jonas' house, where they could see each other. As she sat and watched him, Jack dug out her potatoes and harvested what grain had not fallen off the stem in the fields.

When he finished, he returned to the house, and called her inside to collect all her belongings and gather them into an old towed sack. Then Jack nailed the doors and windows shut on Jonas Barton's house. Lifting the sack to his shoulder, Jack took her hand and brought her to the home where Elmer had once lived, while the valley watched — and wondered.

NELLIE-BOY

She lived by the stars and wind — the logic of her palm
and dark wisdom of plants and insects. Baba-Yaga, we called
her as children. The witch of the hillside. The ugly old
woman.

She lived on a stony bit of sloping ground, in a wooden shack
chinked with mud plaster against the wind and weather. A
squatter she was, paying no rent or taxes. When Bill Sitwell
bought surrounding land for his grain and cattle empire, he
tried to have her removed.

"So long's I live, the land I stand on is me own! Go on —
push down me house — throw me out on the road with me
child — and all your money and machines will not spare you
from destruction, you greedy blackguards!" She shouted at
him.

There was meaning to what she said, like an ancient echo
of a truth long forgotten but still significant to a people who
live off the soil.

So she stood in her yard, defiant — her chin thrust high,
and the grey geese cackling and hissing around her with excitement. Bill Sitwell made no move to enter her house. He lit
a cigarette nervously and retreated, never to bother her again.

The geese she kept, she plucked for feathers. In the autumn

of the year, she sold the feathers for quilt filling in the neighbourhood, and the geese themselves for meat at the local creamery. The rest of the year, she remained confined to her tiny homestead — a stranger in our midst — unknown, mysterious and fearful.

She was supposed to have a child in her house. How old this child was — why she or he was never seen — why the school board did not investigate, was a source of mystery to old and young in the neighbourhood. She paid no visits to her neighbours, and none went to call on her.

But despite her strange isolation, we were aware of her. We drew hideous caricatures of her bedevilled face on the school blackboard. We screeched and chanted dirty couplets at her house when a group of us walked past on the road and felt the courage of a crowd. One summer, young Ted Sitwell killed one of her geese on the road with his bicycle. And Yurie Melnyk, the kid with ears like two dinner plates, threw a stone and broke her window on Hallowe'en night. But the old woman did not complain to our parents about this.

And then there was the evening which will always haunt me — the evening I met Nellie-Boy . . . .

It was stormy, with bursts of rain and fast-driven clouds churning rapidly across the sky. It wasn't cold, but the rain when it came was biting to the cheek, so I kept my head down as I hurried home from the post office. The one letter I held in my pocket had long turned to mush, as had the straw hat I wore on my head.

Because I kept my head low, I didn't see my companion on the road until I was right on her. She was walking in the direction I was going, and hadn't heard me come up.

"Hallow!" I spoke. "Who's this?"

She was shorter and thinner than I. In one hand she carried a dirty canvas bag, half-filled with something and soggy wet. Without turning, she began to run at the sound of my voice. She had no shoes on her feet and she was a fast runner even on the muddy road, but I gave chase. In a few paces I caught her by the shoulder, which felt sharp and thin, through the light, soaked shirt she wore.

"What ya runnin' for?" I turned her roughly around to face me.

"Let me go, boy!"

"Tell me why ya runnin', or I'm gonna whop ya!"

I was still holding on to her, and she turned and cringed back as far as she could from me. She was full of fight, in the wild way of people who wish to stay out of trouble. It was a dangerous, catlike anger — with her large, dark eyes opening and closing as if with a secret pulse of their own. I relaxed my hold.

"Why'd ya run? Who are ya?"

"I wasn't runnin' — can't a soul go fast when I feel like fast?" She replied, her voice rising. I hadn't thought of *her* rights to being on the road, and this stopped me for a moment. She saw me hesitate, and this gave her courage.

"What business ya got holdin' on to me? Lemme go!"

I released her and she stepped out of reach.

"Ya just come here? I never seen ya before." I said flatly.

A fresh rain whipped down suddenly, and she stamped her foot impatiently.

"What ya got in the bag?" I demanded, without waiting for a reply to my first question.

"Me name's Nellie-Boy." She said. "I live there."

She pointed in the direction of the old woman's shack. At first, I didn't connect this kid with the old woman and the kid we'd never seen. I giggled, thinking she was some new family in the neighbourhood, and playing tricks with me. Then a cold sort of fear began to spread through me, and I couldn't giggle any more.

"Ya're lyin'!" I said loudly. "an' what kind of name's Nellie-Boy? Ya ain't no boy!"

"That don't matter — I'm gonna be! Me mother said so!"

There was a fire in her eyes when she spoke and I felt uncomfortable.

Her standing like that before me, with the weedy hills behind her, and dark clouds falling right around her thin shoulders, she became something strange and unwordly. I had to attack, or turn tail and run.

"Your mother!" I spoke harshly. "Your mother ain't the old woman up there, is she?"

Nellie-Boy nodded.

"But ya ain't got no father — what ya talkin' about?" I knew brutal secrets about the ways of life, but here on the deserted road, what I knew seemed of no consequence.

"I don't need no father. I was brought out of the ground, like a pumpkin seed." Nellie-Boy said coldly.

"What ya got in the bag?" I pointed, and Nellie-Boy pulled it behind herself.

"Gimme it!"

She turned and ran, slipping and crouching first, then straightening and moving away with the bag swinging wildly at her side. I went after her, catching the bag before she got more than a dozen steps.

She held tightly, tugging to get it away from me. But I was mad now, and hit her in the face with my fist. She released the bag, blood oozing from her nose, and shaking her head with astonishment she staggered away from me.

Her eyes lit with a terrible fire, and her lips became white and dry with anger. She rushed me suddenly, her little fists raised pathetically. I laughed, and pushed her aside with my shoulder. Then I took the bag by its bottom and poured out its contents on the road.

Mushrooms. Nothing but a bagful of wet, brown mushrooms, which grow in the underbrush during the rainy season here.

"Whyn't ya tell me it was crap? Somebody's think it was gold the way ya carried on!" I tried to sound scolding. Then to impress upon her the degree of my contempt, I trampled the mushrooms into the muddy road until they became an orange slick in the mire.

She didn't fight now. She just stood in front of me, trembling with frustration and rage. Her eyes opened wide. Just then, a cloud passed overhead and a fresh burst of rain pelted us. Her eyes seemed to become the eyes of a giant cat.

"I'll get ya for this!" She hissed in a voice hardly audible above the whisper of the rain. My aggressiveness was gone now, and I felt tired and ashamed. Pushing her aside, I started walking home.

"Here!" I turned and threw the empty bag at her feet. "Pick yourself some more mushrooms. You coulda told me when I asked."

The rain was becoming heavier and the sky darkened as with night. Bending my head low and pulling the dripping collar of my jacket over my neck, I hurried on. I heard her follow behind me — her footsteps squishing in the mud. I bent my head lower and hurried. When next I looked up, she was in front of me. I watched her bare heels sink and rise in the monotonous, wet road. A wind came up, bending the boughs of roadside trees, and twisting her hair around her neck and over her right shoulder. She was drawing away from me, and I hurried, feeling I must not lose her for what road remained for us to walk together.

At the place where the old woman kept her geese, Nellie-Boy stopped and turned to me. I also stopped, keeping my distance, for her face was dark and shadowed with a strange storm of its own.

"I'll tell my mother what you done — she'll fix ya!" she growled, then jumped across the water-swollen ditch and ran up the hillside to the weathered shack of a house. It seemed even more dreary and bleak in the half-light of the rainstorm than it did on other days.

Home was still two miles down the road for me, and I ran now — ran out of fear of Nellie-Boy and her mother — the

Baba-Yaga of the countryside who worshipped strange, black gods. The nameless woman who angered only once, when Bill Sitwell went to evict her from her home . . . . The witch who brought Nellie-Boy to life from a pumpkin seed . . . .

The years pass and one forgets the over-real fears and prejudices of childhood. My father sold his farm to Bill Sitwell, and we left the countryside for the city. This was my break with the soil, with childhood — with the nobility and foolishness of the earth and all its terrible passions. In the schools and streets of my new environment I became a reasoning man.

Yet a memory and a guilt persisted, even when I thought I had forgotten . . . .

I was in my second year as an electrical apprentice, when I decided to make a return visit to the place of my birth. My father still had to collect a mortgage payment from Bill Sitwell, and I accompanied him out.

It was a peaceful June morning when we drove — one of those happy mornings in spring when you see wild roses at the roadside opening their hearts to the sun. There were sounds of sun in the air, and the smell of wild grass and dead seasons. I remembered all this, and my blood warmed with excitement and interest.

An hour later, my father slowed the car and pointed.

"Look! Remember the old woman's shack? Wonder why Bill didn't push it down . . . Cripes! There's still someone there — look at those geese!"

And I sat upright, rigid as a board.

"Wait!" I said, catching hold of his arm. "Let me off here. I . . . I want to walk a bit. Car ride's making me dizzy. Pick me up on your way back. I'll be on the road."

"Bill Sitwell ain't seen ya since you were this high." My father argued.

"Let me off!" I spoke sharply now, and he pressed the brakes hard.

We had passed the old woman's shack, and I turned my head

to keep it in view. I waited until my father drove around the first bend in the road. Then I hesitantly made my way to the grey building on the hill.

The mottled geese raised their long necks and hissed at me as I approached. I looked around, studying the house and the small bit of land closely. The only changes I noticed were the changes wrought by time. The window Yurie Melnyk had broken was never replaced. Cardboard had been stuck behind the pane, and now even that cardboard had rotted, and still another one was placed behind the first to support it. The shack was listing to one side, and the wood was furry with weathering.

I knocked on the door, and it rattled on loose hinges. There was no sign of life in the building, so I knocked again, more loudly. The geese began to cackle alarmingly, and close in a circle around me. I began to feel hot and short of breath. Doubts and childlike fears I had long forgotten began crowding me into a small, cowardly part of my being.

"Shut up!" I shouted at the milling, roused geese — and I knocked again. Then I opened the door, and poked my head into the dark room. The smell of poverty — the poignant odour of old cloth, cheap soap and leftover food struck me in the face and I retreated. It was the smell of my youth — of all things I had ever known. It was the smell that ferments the goodness out of a man, leaving a shell of humanity that survives with its own peculiar bruises.

I struggled for reason and caught it as I closed the door of the shack and hesitated on the brink of some other time. I was conscious for the first time of my tasteful clothing and finely polished shoes. But I was out of place here. I wanted to roll in the dirt — scratch earth into my hair — and so have the hissing geese know me and leave me in peace. They were low at my heels now, their wings and necks poised to strike.

"Hish!" A sharp, thin voice cried, and instantly the geese became silent and retreated from me, walking backwards. I looked up, and saw her, standing, leaning with one withered arm against the corner of the cabin.

"Nellie-Boy!" I cried, and then I hesitated, for I was no longer certain. She was tiny — a stunted child in height, but her face was an unforgettable mask of hunger, despair, pain. It was an ugly face, with hooked nose, bad teeth, and waxen, crinkled skin. It was the face of an old woman — but not the old woman I had seen in my crass childhood — for in this face the lines and ravages were my work, the work of Bill Sitwell and his young boy Ted, of Yurie Melnyk, and all the others. I stared at her.

"What the hell ya want?" Her voice was shrill, almost a shout.

"You know me, Nellie-Boy." I began hesitantly, in a cracked tone I could not relax. "I used to live a couple of miles down the road. You remember that evening on the road when I dumped your mushrooms into the mud — a couple of crazy kids we were then, eh . . ."

I thought I saw her eyes widen ever so slightly with returning memory — but if she remembered, she said nothing. Just stood there, one arm resting on the shack corner, staring hostilely at me. I had to talk, make her understand I meant no harm.

"You must remember . . . how you told me you came to life from the earth, like a pumpkin seed — you remember that, don't you?" I was getting desperate to communicate with her, for I noticed the geese stop in their retreat and crane their necks angrily at me again. "You even told me how you knew you'd become a boy in time, because your mother said so. Now there may be something in that — science is discovering much more in primitive faith than was the case in the past . . ."

Still the same stare — not a muscle moving, not a flutter in her dismally tattered clothes.

"Look!" I blurted. "I can't make up for the hurt I done you then, but I got ten or fifteen bucks on me. Here, take

157

them and buy yourself and your mother something nice. I'm sorry for what I done."

I reached out to her with the money in my hand. Deliberately, as if it was all part of a rehearsed ritual, she lowered her hand from the wall, then bending forward ever so slightly, spat directly into my face. Instinctively I raised my arm and slapped her so hard her head collided with a dull thud against the shack before she fell in a grotesque heap to the ground.

And an hour later, still running frantically down the road, I prayed — yes, I prayed aloud, for the powers above to wilt my arm from my body, or have the earth open before me, so I could fall face down and be devoured by more worthy life than my own . . . .

HALF-CASTE

We had always known each other. There had never been a time when it was otherwise. I was not aware of intentional plans for our meetings, but we met frequently and in different parts of the city. And when we met, he would run his long, black fingers into my hair and jiggle my head playfully.

"You been taken care of good?" he would ask, and I would reply that I was.

We met in vacant lots behind warehouse buildings, in hard-to-reach places in parks, and out of town on railway sidings. Sometimes he would have a crushed chocolate bar to give me, and as I munched, he told me stories out of his past — never the present — but out of a past which seemed long departed. Of men he worked with, travelled with — yes, and fought with.

"Nobody ever pushed this old man around! No sirree . . . ," and he would slap one fist into the open palm of his other hand.

I knew him and never questioned his stories. And a long time before, I learned not to speak to my mother of meeting him. She spanked me the first time — spanked me so hard I slept on my stomach three nights.

"Look at you!" She had said. "Look in the mirror! You look like me . . . like all them blond kids on the street! What's the matter with you, boy? You want shit thrown at you?"

So we met in out-of-the-way places — again not intentionally — but it seemed both of us knew we must not be seen together. He told me his stories, fidgeting with his hands while he spoke, or stretching out his long, angular body on the grass and talking with a bashed-up hat over his face. When it got late, he would send me home.

"Oh, I got something here for you," he would say first. Then he would fumble in his pockets and pull out money — always paper money, tied in a roll with shop-string. "Give it to your mother . . ."

When I told her of the first meeting, she spanked me. After that, she said nothing — not even when I gave her the money without explanation. We were too poor for more than a show of pride.

I saw a man like him whipped once, in Halifax, in the light of day. A group of fat, blond men pulled up in front of the run-down house we lived in then. They must have reckoned the house vacant — it looked vacant from the outside, but I was there, watching through a broken window. They pulled him out of their car and bull-whipped him in the overgrown front yard. He didn't holler, but I saw his dark skin crack where they'd torn his shirt off — and the blood shoot out like it was compressed in him. Then they threw him down, and drove away in a hurry. I didn't wake my mother, and I didn't go out to help. The next day, he wasn't there anymore.

. . . He gave me money, tightly rolled and tied with shop-string. It was never enough, and when I told him we had gone on welfare, he left greasy brown paper bags filled with cold roasted ribs and cut-up chicken, as well as money.

"You work in a cafe?" I asked him, but he pretended not to hear. Or maybe he was thinking a lot, for he seemed so sad that day. He sighed and paced back and forth — then sent me home early.

Welfare cut us off, and we had to move. I asked my mother why. She laughed the laugh that begins and ends in the nose, but she did not explain. Even when she did answer a question, it was never an answer, for she spoke oddly — even to the welfare people. She spoke like the spatterings of a paint brush — not enough to mean anything — just random spots of truth covering something else. One social worker, a thin man with bad teeth and eczema over one eyelid, once asked her when she was born.

"When I shouldn't have been," she replied. He chuckled, and as he left the house, he pinched her on the stomach, just below her breast. She said ouch, and he laughed a whistling sort of giggle, his shoulders hunched and quivering . . . .

We were given a train ticket for a long ride to Calgary. With what money we had left, she had her hair curled and then found a job as char-woman at the Palizer hotel. That night, in a one-room basement place she rented for ten dollars a month, she kissed me and danced with me.

"We're new! Nobody to know us, an' nobody to spit on us! We'll make it go!" She danced and laughed until she was out of breath. I didn't know what *it* was, or where *go* would take us.

Within a month, she bought a mattress for the floor, and two chairs, off which we ate, and on which we sat listening to the radio at night. Pots lay in a corner unwashed — palpitating singers whined cowboy love songs and top-fifty hits — naked drainpipes down our east wall gurgled from the toilet upstairs. She sat with her eyes closed right into the night, rocking to some rhythm I could not hear. Upstairs, the landlord argued with his wife and the television played full volume, nobody listening. In the mornings, the landlord woke us by spattering gravel against our window with his car tires as he drove away . . . .

Three more years, and I was ten. We were still in the same basement, but now we had furniture. No rooms. But furniture set up in four separate parts of the basement, as if walls divided each section. We had a poplin curtain on the driveway window, which had numerous gravel breaks in it now. She was too shy to demand new glass from the landlord. Still the television upstairs played at full volume, and the people fought. But my mother was fatter, and I had a newspaper route which paid twelve dollars a week.

He didn't appear all this time. We had lost him, or he had lost us. I thought about him, but only on Sundays when I had nothing to do but walk around, kicking bits of rubbish and pebbles, looking into soaped windows of new buildings, or balancing precariously over an open excavation where workmen installed sewers and gaslines during working weekdays. I would often walk right out of town to the hillside overlooking Montgomery — and there in the lonely, windswept spaces I would remember him, and look around for a sight of him. But he didn't come.

There came a time when my mother was dismissed from her job. That weekend, she came down with the flu, and found herself a boyfriend. He was, like other friends of hers, heavy on the bottom and overdressed. When I came home after finishing my Saturday paper route, he was already there, well into a second bottle of whiskey. He looked at me with half-shut eyes. Mother was sitting on a chair in another section of the basement, shouting drunk.

"Get this pig out of here! Throw him out, Son!"

I looked at the man, and his lips jiggled with a crooked smile. He pursed his mouth at me and took another sip from his bottle. I was so hungry I was hurting inside . . . .

"Come on, Son! Throw him out — he's no good! Where are you going? Obey your mother!"

"Listen to your maw, damn you!" I heard the stud bellow as I left the house.

On the street, I met Jimmy and Mike — two kids from the basement across the road. Jimmy was my age — taller than me by an inch, but with a queered shoulder. He'd fallen off a construction scaffold once, breaking his shoulder blade, which was allowed to heal without setting. It healed crooked.

Mike was two years younger. He had adenoids bad, which gave him a whine going clear through his personality. His mom fed him raw onions for his adenoids, and his breath smelled like an open sewer.

They began walking with me. We walked into the sunset, away from the squalid, low buildings which went underground for another story, as concrete was cheaper than wood in this city. We reached the downtown area — and the soulless crowd which herded and broke apart at shop doorways and intersection lights.

Mike spotted a new Ford, and making a soft grunting sound, traced its outline with a finger on the wind.

"Where are we going?" Jimmy asked. I said nowhere, and he was content. A conceited smile crossed his lips. "I know a secret cave under the bridge," he said. We turned off the main avenue into a side street of bakeshops and meat stores. The smell of fried meat became an explosion of saliva in my mouth. I fingered the paper-route collections in my pocket, and pushed open the first door, buying Jimmy and myself a hot-dog each and a cinnamon bun for Mike. We went out, stopping just outside the doorway to eat.

Shops were beginning to darken inside. I saw our reflections dance over the plate glass windows we passed — Jimmy and I together and Mike behind, just meeting his own image on the glass as we broke contact with ours.

"Where's this cave?"

"You promise not to tell?"

"Promise!"

Jimmy led the way now, talking over his shoulder about a real live cowpoke by the name of Chuck, whom he met at last year's stampede. Chuck had even shared a plate of flapjacks with Jimmy. But when I asked, he couldn't remember if he'd eaten them with butter or maple syrup . . . .

From behind, Mike followed with a story of a bronco he had seen at the same time. Mike was a painfully slow talker. I could anticipate his story a minute before his telling, and it made my neck itch.

"Bronc could sure jump high . . ."

"As high as a trolley-line?" I asked.

"How'd you know?" Mike's cinnamon-stained lips drooped in a sulk.

There was a path under the bridge. It led to a grassy hollow of river silt, deepened mysteriously by the low sun.

I saw him! I saw him there in the hollow. Bent, bare headed, completely grey now, crushed by the same three years that had lifted and stretched my own frame. He was carrying a tin of water up from the river. But the cry of recognition that welled in my throat did not get through my lips. Instead . . . .

"Hey! Lookit that black bum!"

Jimmy and Mike saw him, and they nudged me to stop. Jimmy's face lit with terrible mischief.

"Hey — let's scat under the bridge where he don't see us, then come runnin' at him screaming murder! Let's throw some stones at 'im too! Give 'im a good scare! The dirty, thievin' bum!"

They ran from me, their feet silent in the long grass.

I kept walking towards him — so far towards him, but he didn't look up to see me. He carried his overflowing tin, slowly, head down, going to some destination known only to himself. Then I could go no further, neither could I turn away from him. He came so near I could see the spiralling wrinkles on his cheeks, where death had already set in. He looked up.

Even as his eyes struggled with recognition, a big, sudden smile warmed his tired face. He dropped his water tin and stumbled to me, his arms outstretched.

"Lord! Lordy! Son — you tracking me, or me tracking you — how is it? Your mommy all right? Lordy, but you've grown! Let me squeeze you like I used to! It's been a long time . . . everywhere I've looked. Nothin' . . . nothin' left but lookin' . . ."

164

From under the bridge, the boys came at a gallop, hollering like they had planned to. Then they saw me, my face buried in the sour cloth of the old man's coat.

"Let 'im go — you bad man! Run, Mike! Call the police!"

He stepped back when he heard the shouts, his face twisted with surprise and hurt.

"Don't call no police! I didn't hurt him, boys . . ."

He looked to me to explain to Jimmy and Mike. I couldn't move. I couldn't say anything. I just saw his dark eyes — the colour of the land and all storms above the land. Eyes bleached and stained by the sun and sorrow. My head dropped and his hands came into focus . . . hands swollen by hunger and shaking with arthritis and fear . . . hands suddenly rising and clutching at the collar of his shirt as if his exposed neck was the one vulnerable spot on his body. I looked up. Words were being shaped by his parched old lips, but I heard no sound.

"Run, Mike! Call the police!"

His eyes opened wide with disbelief and he began to tremble all over.

"No!"

His shout was the agony of a spirit being torn away from its flesh. I heard the boys break away and run for help, their footsteps a malicious whisper dying in the grass.

"No!" He shouted again.

Turning from him, I doubled over and fled . . . .

All the shop windows past which I ran in my life were mirrors of my image — firm Nordic chin and nose moving smoothly over glass. Blond, uncut hair blowing in the wind — skimming over merchandise behind the windows. I had etched out patterns of responsibility over the glass windows of the city, newspaper bag over my shoulder — running forward between him and her. Now, the newspaper bag was all I could carry — my share of rent and friendship, and support for her, the living parent.

"Boys! Don't call the cops!" His piping voice wailed from

the hollow. "I'll give you a nickel each if you stop running! I thought he was somebody I knowed . . ."

Two more years I carried the paper-route . . . returning at nights to the same basement, the same open sham of a home. The studmen multiplied now, coming and going, and the frequency of her interviews for work became more rare. Then one took her away. By now the boys across the street had figured it out, and the distance between us became more than the width of a street.

I began moving from city to city — as he had done before. But now I am searching for him. It will be too late to help when I do find him — but I wish to be there when he dies — to give him peace in knowing I remembered his stories behind warehouses, down railway tracks, and in the parks . . . the tight little rolls of money . . . brown paper bags of sandwiches and cold roasted ribs . . . the life he never had for being near us and guarding us in his own way.

I want to be there, so I can tell my children when they are born looking like him.

BIRTH OF A PLAYWRIGHT: TWO EARLY SCRIPTS

VILLAGE CROSSROAD

Cast

HAROLD: 20-year-old quarry hand. Sturdy, but physically damaged from motorcycle accident injuries. His memory has been disturbed, and his reactions tend to be hesitant and uncertain.

MARGIE: About the same age as Harold. She lives with her parents on a farm, but is employed as housekeeper for the schoolteacher's family in the village.

JOEY: Slightly younger, and a leader of the village "gang." A restless, brutal youth.

3 BOYS: Various ages and backgrounds. Followers of Joey.

Scene

Crossroad short of the village. There are lamp-posts alongside of the road. Wooden boardwalk from the village ends at the crossroads, where the village road is intercepted by road leading to the quarry. A few trees line the roads. Behind are fruit and grain farms. Dust everywhere and hot sun. In the distance, periodic muffled explosions from the quarry.

ON CAMERA: *HAROLD is waiting, awkwardly leaning on a fence which runs parallel with the road to the village. He is dressed in his work overalls, and his face is smudged with quarry dirt. In his hands he holds a paper bag which he twists and squeezes impatiently.*

MARGIE, neatly dressed, approaches on her way to the village. She pauses at the crossroads, looks in the direction of the quarry, then crosses to where HAROLD is waiting.

HAROLD: Gee, Margie! I been waiting an hour for ya. Where ya been so long?

MARGIE: (*testily*) What's it to ya! Ya get paid yet?

HAROLD: Yep. Got something for ya.

MARGIE: Show me watcha got.

HAROLD: (*playfully*) Whatcha gonna give me in return?

MARGIE: A kick where'll hurt, if ya don't watch out. Whatcha get me? (*grabs the bag from HAROLD's hands*)

HAROLD: I was gonna get it wrapped nice in a box like they have it in the store window, but I didn't have time. I thought you was gonna be early, maybe.

MARGIE: (*pearing into bag and screwing up her face*) Oranges and a couple rotten bananas! Jesus, but your cheap! Ya'd think

I was a kid or something. Why doncha get me a lollypop. It'd cost ya less!

HAROLD: (*upset*) I'm sorry, Margie. I just ran over to Sid's store — couldn't get my cheque cashed or anything. Sid borrowed me some cash till tomorrow. There wasn't much of anything nice in the store, though.

MARGIE: (*biting into an orange, peel and all*) Sharrup! Sharrup! How much did they pay ya?

HAROLD: Just ninety-five bucks. I been off a lot with my back.

MARGIE: Ya got no kicks. I'm healthy, an' I only make twenty a week and one lunch a day at Sinclair's. A lousy cheese sandwich on brown bread and a glass of milk. They don't eat no meat at Sinclair's — they're the kind of people that don't ever eat no meat. Sure could go a baloney sandwich sometimes. Mr. Sinclair says you are what ya eat. Do you think if I eat enough of their lousy cheese sandwiches I'll become a lousy cheese myself?

HAROLD: I dunno. (*kicks at pebble*). Margie, I been meaning to ask ya something. The other boys makes more shovelling lime, and the boss says I gotta work as hard as they to keep up, or he'll let me go. It ain't easy, Margie. My back gives me hell, and sometimes I just forget what I'm doin' . . . and . . . Margie, what was it like before I cracked up?

MARGIE: (*thinking*) Ya weren't as cheap as ya are now. I dunno — ya were a lot of fun, and nobody didn't poke no fingers at ya without getting them smashed. Ya looked different, that's all. Ya weren't twisted up like yore side was roped. (*angrily*) What the hell difference does it make anyhow? Ya wanna banana?

HAROLD: They never called me a kook before, did they? Tell me, Margie — did they?

MARGIE: Aw, pipe down! Leave me alone! I gotta go sweep up Mrs. Sinclair's house and wash her dishes.

HAROLD: I'll walk to the village with ya, Margie.

MARGIE: Ya think I'm crazy? I mean . . . ya walk so slow, and I'm late. See you around — in the funny-pictures, maybe! (*starts to leave*)

HAROLD: Wait, Margie! I was savin' something special for ya. Ya won't be working late, and I'm off for the day. I was gonna go home an' change — and then, I want to take ya to the pictures. How about it, Margie?

MARGIE: (*startled*) No! No — I gotta work late, Harold. Then I gotta go home an' hem some skirts for the old lady. I dunno why — with her varicose veins, she should wear slacks to bed. No, Harold. Maybe next payday.

HAROLD: Okay, Margie. Okay. (*feigns cheerfulness*) I'll dud up anyhow, and take one of my friends to the show!

MARGIE: Friends? You ain't got no friends, Harold. You ain't got a friend in all creation. See you later, alligator — an' thanks for the lousy oranges!

Fade

ON CAMERA: *Same set as previous scene. It is evening of same day, and the roads are deserted. A boy on bicycle appears, riding to the village. He sings a few bars of "Zing! Went the Strings*

172

*of My Heart" and disappears. Approaching from uproad,
HAROLD appears. When he reaches the boardwalk, he stops
to dust his shoes with a handkerchief. HAROLD is dressed for
"going out" and bareheaded. He looks back in the direction from
which he came, and thinks with open-mouthed concentration.
A few sharp blasts of a car-horn sound from the direction of the
quarry, and in moments a jalopy approaches. Without slowing,
it makes a skidding turn into the village road. JOEY, the driver,
and his three young passengers, see HAROLD. They shout, and
stopping the car, reverse it and make a noisy return to where
HAROLD is standing.*

1st BOY: I thought it was a tree!

2nd BOY: An' I thought it was superman!

3rd BOY: Crackies! Are ya guys blind? It's the kook! Hiya,
kook!

JOEY: Shut up, ya guys! Shut up, or ya can start walking!
(*to HAROLD*) Wanna lift, old boy?

HAROLD: No, thanks. I got lotsa time.

1st BOY: He's got lotsa time! Ask him if he got lotsa money!

JOEY: Shut up! (*to HAROLD*) Hey, don't get sore at us.
The boys are a little high and silly, but they mean well. Would
ya like a little snort with us?

HAROLD: (*Approaches. He is puzzled*) I'm all right. Everything's all right.

JOEY: We know everything's all right, old boy. Would ya like a small snort — a bit of a drink? (*offers bottle from breast pocket of jacket*)

HAROLD: (*shakes his head*) I don't touch the stuff.

2nd BOY: We don't touch it neither — we just drink it!

JOEY: Now come on, Harold — we're just being friendly. We like our pals to have a drink with us, and maybe sometime ya can return the favour. Don't be hard to get along with, or we're bound to get sore at ya. Whatya say, Harold? A small snort? (*Leans over and holds bottle under HAROLD's nose*)

3rd BOY: C'mon, Joey. Don't waste likker. No tellin' what the kook'll do when he gets loaded.

Turning sharply, JOEY slaps the boy hard across the mouth.

JOEY: (*threateningly*) Don't nobody call my pal bad names! He was a great guy before he got hurt. Used to get anything he wanted — all the likker — all the dames — all the best-paying jobs on tobacco. Used to be a real hopping dump here when Harold was the big boy!

HAROLD: Did I really do all them things, Joey? (*takes a drink*)

JOEY: Sure, kid, sure! Ya were my idol then. Ya had this big Harley-Davidson bike — cripes! That thing could do ninety goin' uphill! A beaut it was! And there was this chick — Katy Dixon — a real dish! Her old man used to run a fleet of trucks between Toronto and Sudbury. The summer she came out to work on tobacco for the heck of it, she stuck on to ya. Used to sit on the back of yar bike, screaming hard as she could when ya throttled it to a cool eighty-five on these country roads!

Ya were a big guy in them days, Harold, an' I'm still glad to be yore pal! Have another — it's on Joey!

HAROLD: (*takes another drink and coughs*) Gee, it's awful nice of ya to stop, Joey. Ya know what I was gonna do tonight?

1st BOY: (*smugly*) Naw — tell us. (*JOEY jabs him in the ribs threateningly*)

HAROLD: I was gonna go see the pictures! Ain't been to a picture since April. I seen where Alan Ladd is playing in this here picture in the village — should be something to see! (*He is still holding the bottle, which he stares at.*)

JOEY: Go ahead, pal — have another. Ya can pay Joey back sometime. Ya gonna see a picture alone?

HAROLD: Yeh. Too late to ask anybody.

JOEY: Can't ya get a dame to go? Boys been telling me they seen ya buying things to eat for Margie Miller. Me, I got nothin' against Margie — but she just don't fit into no gang. Feed her is about all a guy can do — ya can't talk to her. Her voice is like a church bell — ya can hear her a mile, and everything she says is dirty. It ain't right to be seen with a dame like her, Harold — just a walking feedbag and bust as the day she was born. Must keep you broke to give her the grub she likes.

HAROLD: Tain't so! She don't eat that much. Don't say nothin' bad about Margie — she's my friend!

JOEY: (*raising his hands*) No hard feelings, old boy. No hard feelings. As I say, I don't know the girl — I got nothin' against her. But you could do better!

175

HAROLD: No I couldn't! Even she . . . aw, forget it.

JOEY: (*pretending sympathy*) Did ya ask Margie to go see the movies with ya?

HAROLD: (*nodding*) Yeh . . . yeh, I did.

JOEY: An' she stood ya up?

HAROLD: No! 'Tain't so! She had work to do at home — said she had to hem her old lady's skirts, or something. Gee, I can't remember — I'm sorta dizzy.

JOEY: (*angrily*) Did ya hear that, fellas? Margie Miller stood him up! What kinda dame stands our pal up? What we gonna do about a dame like that?

1st BOY: We'll rough her old man up some!

2nd BOY: Hell! Let's go burn his damned house down!

HAROLD: No! Stop it! Even if she did stand me up, it's my business, not yours!

JOEY: Now, now Harold — don't get sore at your pals. We're only tryin' to help.

HAROLD: (*passes back bottle to JOEY*) Thanks. But I don't need help.

JOEY: Look, Harold — we're sorry — really. But let me give ya some advice. That twisted up shoulder, and all them things ya can't remember — that don't mean nothin' to us. Ya can still be one of the gang and go on all the larks and good times. But ya gotta stand up on yore hind legs. Ya gotta be a man again. Betcha anything, Margie will be walking down the road now on her way to the village. She always goes to the village in the evenings. There's nothing else to do. Now ya wait, and when ya see her, ya just tell her — don't go askin' her — tell her she's goin' to the pictures with ya — and ya'll see what that does.

HAROLD: (*uncertainly*) What if she says, no? She don't want to be seen with me where there's people. (*inadvertently glances at his deformed shoulder*)

JOEY: Then ya just haul off an' paste her one on the kisser! No dame is big enough to lead a guy around by the nose. Ya spent enough on her, aintcha? Whatcha want to do — get down on yore hands and knees in front of her? Ya just stand up to her, an' she'll be eating outa yore hands. Ya'll see. S'long pal!

JOEY starts the jalopy and backs it around the crossroad. When he is on the quarry road just around the corner, he stops the motor. Sounds of laughter from the gang can be heard. HAROLD rubs his fingers over his eyes, then clutches his head. A moment later, MARGIE appears walking from uproad in direction of village. JOEY's gang honk the horn at her, and she grins and waves back. Wolf-whistles and muffled comments from the gang, and she swells with pride.

MARGIE: (*sees HAROLD and stops short of him*) What's the matter? Ya got no home?

HAROLD: (*uncovers his face and lowers his head menacingly*) Sure, I got a home. I got a bigger home than ya got!

MARGIE: Then ya got no bed.

HAROLD: I got so!

MARGIE: The government built this sidewalk. (*motions HAROLD to step aside*)

HAROLD: I thought ya said ya was gonna sew up skirts for your old woman. That's why ya wasn't gonna see the pictures with me.

MARGIE: (*defensively*) Well — I sewed them already.

HAROLD: Then we going out together like I asked?

MARGIE: You go fly a kite, ya twisted up, stupid kook! Whatcha take me for? Ya think I got nobody to go out with — ya want everybody to laugh at me?

HAROLD: I thought ya was my friend! I woulda done anything ya asked me! Yore no good — yore just a . . . just a feedbag! (*Approaches as if to strike her. MARGIE steps back a pace, then stiffens.*)

MARGIE: You! Hah! Ya gonna hit a woman 'cause ya ain't got guts or brains left to stand up to any man! (*thrusts out chin*) C'mon then — show me how big an' handy ya are! C'mon — maybe it'll make ya feel better for each time a two-bit straw-boss an' small-town punk makes a floor mat outa ya! C'mon — hit me, if that's what yore aimin' to do!

HAROLD: (*drops his hand*) I . . . I can't hit ya, Margie.

MARGIE: Ya ain't got the nerve to hit me, kook?

HAROLD: No, no, Margie — it ain't nerve that's missing. I can't remember . . . (*laughter in background*) Joey's wrong, that's all.

MARGIE: (*hears laughter*) Joey? What's that creep got to do with ya?

HAROLD: (*rubbing forehead in confusion*) He drove by and gave me a drink — I shouldna drunk it. He told me about myself — what I used to be. (*looks at MARGIE appealingly*) Margie — is it true? Where's it all gone? He told me to stand up to ya — to get off my knees an' tell ya what I wanted . . . what I need . . .

Laughter in background. MARGIE hears and smiles.

MARGIE: So Joey figures yore too big for Margie? Don't ya go listening to those creeps, Harold. (*pauses and considers*) Harold, I ain't never had nobody ask me proper for a date. Now if you was to ask me — like, like they do in them pictures — I mean, real nice. Harold — who knows, I might just do it — ya, even more I might do! It ain't no way to ask Margie by tryin' to hit her. Why don't ya ask me on yore knees, Harold? C'mon — there ain't nobody to see! C'mon, Harold, it ain't hard. Yore just muddled up, that's all.

HAROLD: (*Brushes his face awkwardly with his hand and looks around him, then lowers himself on his knees before her.*) Like this, Margie? Is this what ya want?

MARGIE: Yes, Harold — yes! Take me around the knees with yore hands, Harold. That's right. Ask me now, Harold . . .

HAROLD: Gee, Margie — come to the pictures, will ya, please?

MARGIE: (*loudly, with face turned to the crossroads*) Hey, Joey! Fellas! Come see this guy! Come see old kook here!

179

Laughing, the gang emerges on foot and surrounds HAROLD and MARGIE. HAROLD, stunned, continues kneeling, holding on to MARGIE.

JOEY: (*pulling HAROLD's arms away*) Well, look at this, willya! The big, strong Harold! I used to look up to ya once, old boy. Ya sure have gone to hell — ya sure have. (*eyes MARGIE appreciatively*) Ya're sure some girlie to do this to the kook! Dolls like ya need me with guts — lotsa guts!

MARGIE: (*grins*) Get off it. Yore saying that for kicks.

JOEY: (*With mock seriousness*) Come off it, Margie! We mean it. Dolls like ya are hard to get. Ya deserve a break, kid. How's about me and the boys takin' ya out and showing ya a real good time? Whatya say, Margie?

MARGIE: Well, I dunno. Ya going to the pictures?

JOEY: Pictures? Oh, sure! We'll go to the pictures. Fellas! Ya hear? We're going to the pictures! Sure — we'll go anywhere ya like, Margie — you've proven your one of the boys!

HAROLD: (*still on his knees*) Margie! Don't ya listen to them! Don't go anywhere with them!

1st BOY: (*rushing at HAROLD*) Shutup, kook!

MARGIE: (*throwing her hips*) For Christ's sake, stop yore bellyaching, kook! I'm free, white, and old enough. When I wanna go, I go!

JOEY: That's our speed, Margie, doll!

She links arms with JOEY and they walk in direction of the car. HAROLD is still on his knees. 1st BOY approaches and impulsively kicks him hard, knocking HAROLD forward on the walk. The gang laugh and move off after JOEY and MARGIE. HAROLD places his hands over the back of his head, and still lying on the walk, rocks back and forth and convulses with weeping. Sound of car starting and driving away with screeching tires.

Fade

ON CAMERA: Scene opens on same set as previously. It is much later the same night. Sounds of frogs croaking. HAROLD is shaded from the street-lamp by sitting under the fence beneath the branches of an overhanging willow. He is dejected and deep in thought. Sounds of motor, loud laughter, and shouting. JOEY's jalopy appears on night road in the distance, lights on and weaving precariously from one side of the road to the other. Sound of MARGIE's voice shouting in protest. Jalopy approaches and stops opposite where HAROLD is seated, but he is not seen clearly by anyone. One of the boys is draped over the rumble seat of car, and sound asleep. JOEY and the others are drunk.

JOEY: (*voice thick with drink*) There ya are, hell-cat! Joey always brings them back to where he got them. Thanks fer the fun — and don't take no wooden nickels! (*Opens car door and pushes MARGIE out. She is bleeding from facial cuts — her hair dishevelled and clothes torn. Car lurches away. JOEY starts to sing "You Ain't Nothin' But A Hound Dog."*)

MARGIE: (*spitting after car and shaking an upraised fist*) Rotten, dirty pigs! (*attempts to straighten out her clothes*) Oh my God! Oh my God! Pa'll kill me when he finds out!

Stealthily, HAROLD rises to his feet. His face is drawn and intense as he approaches MARGIE silently. Suddenly, she senses him. Bringing her hands up to her mouth, she chokes a scream. HAROLD raises his hand, fist clutched hard, and comes nearer. MARGIE backs away and accidentally gets trapped between the fence and the willow tree.

MARGIE: No, Harold — no! Don't hurt me, please, Harold — I been hurt enough tonight!

Poised over her, HAROLD is frightening in his grim study of her — his eyes dilating and closing. Recollection suddenly seems to come to him, and his face softens with compassion. His fist unclenches, and his fingers reach out to touch a cut on her cheek. Overwhelmed, MARGIE breaks down and cries.

The End

Storm

Cast

MOTHER — Woman in her mid-thirties. She is large with child.

JIMMY — Her son. Between 12 and 14 years of age.

Setting

Farm kitchen of isolated country home. Back and to left of stage is wood-burning stove of previous era. Rough woodbox alongside of stove. Kitchen cupboards and counter run along remaining back wall. Kitchen table and three chairs in centre stage. Left stage is door leading to outside porch. Window on that wall. Right stage is door opening to other rooms of house. This door is partially opened to circulate warmth. Kitchen walls are roughly papered and peeling. A hanging electric bulb with slip-on shade lights the kitchen.

Curtain up on JIMMY, sitting at kitchen table, doing homework. MOTHER is leaning with one arm on counter behind him, staring blankly at window across room. Sounds of wind and storm heard from outside throughout play.

JIMMY: What's the square root of ninety?

MOTHER: Figure it out yourself. I'm no Einstein.

JIMMY: Bet you never took square roots in school.

MOTHER: So — that don't stop me from livin'. My father added by counting on his fingers — but he could tell how many bushels a grainary held just by lookin' at it!

JIMMY: He couldn't!

MOTHER: He could so — so watch what you're sayin'!

JIMMY: Nobody thought to prove him wrong, so you think he was always right, that's all . . .

MOTHER: He LIVED — didn't he? What time is it?

JIMMY: Dunno.

MOTHER: Go an' look, will you? You need a father what stays home, boy — a father who's big enough to take a stick or fist to you. I'm warning you — I'm awful sick, an' not putting up with any more back-talk!

JIMMY: (*rising*) Okay, Mom — I'll look. (*remembers*) Won't do no good. Clock hasn't run all day — I forgot to wind it last night.

MOTHER: You forgot to wind it last night! What's it doing in your room, anyway? You a pack rat? You never had anything of your own? Tell me.

JIMMY: Mom — take another aspirin . . .

MOTHER: Take an aspirin yourself, damn you! I wished you'd been in school instead of bugging me all day — what's the matter with you anyway? Why are you in my hair all the time?

JIMMY: It's not my fault . . .

MOTHER: Your fault what?

JIMMY: About the clock. I thought I would wake up myself so you could sleep some more. But when it started blowing up yesterday, I guess I forgot . . .

MOTHER: It's all right — it don't matter — only how are we going to tell the time?

JIMMY: Heck, Mom — it don't matter.

MOTHER: It don't matter? How am I going to get you off to school on time?

JIMMY: Won't be no school. Roads are drifted level with the fence.

MOTHER: Well, they won't be tomorrow. The snowplow is sure to come through tonight . . .

JIMMY: I don't know. They'd been here now if they'd started off from town this morning.

MOTHER: They're on the way! Just get that into your head — they're on the way! They gotta be!

JIMMY: (*quietly*) Maybe they're not.

MOTHER: What's that?

JIMMY: Nothin'.

MOTHER: It better be nothin! (*walks to window and rubs at ice with finger*) Wind, snow and night. It's black as death out there. Why doesn't something happen? Why doesn't he come home? Two weeks holidays, and he's buggered away the first day already! Bet he's in the beer parlor, drinking it up with that bum, Steve Fedora — throwing his holiday pay around like it was water! I can just hear him — drink up, you guys — it's on me! Work in a mine and keep a farm, an' you're never short of money or grub! As if that was all to life . . .

JIMMY: Can you make me a sandwich, Mom?

MOTHER: Finish your homework first.

JIMMY: I don't have to do this — I'm just workin' ahead.

MOTHER: Were you on the road before you came in?

JIMMY: Uh, huh.

MOTHER: An' you didn't see the snowplow around Williams' farm?

JIMMY: Couldn't see the Williams' farm it's blowing that hard.

MOTHER: I just bet you looked real hard! (*walks back to counter and glances at woodbox*) We'll need another armload of wood for the night. You gonna get it, or do I have to go out?

JIMMY: (*sighs and folds up schoolwork*) Okay . . . I'll go.

MOTHER: Don't have to if it's going to break your back. The way you carry on it's as if I was asking you to go through fire for me.

JIMMY: I don't mind — really I don't! It's just . . .

MOTHER: Just what?

JIMMY: I wish you'd go to bed if you're not feelin' well. I'll stay up an' wait for Dad if he comes.

MOTHER: (*angrily*) Well he's not comin' — you understand! He's not comin' because I need him! You think the storm is holding him back? Nothin' doing! He's celebratin' — doesn't even know I'm waiting! He's out there in the world where there are people, doin' thins, talkin' to one another — loving and laughing. We're a couple of . . . DP's . . . somebody he sends a chunk of his paycheque to — to pay off his damned farm and keep the homefire burning when he has a hunch to drop in! That's your old man, an' don't you forget it!

JIMMY: (*defensively*) You're jus' sayin' that, and you know it ain't so! You're just sayin' that because you're scared mad, that's why!

MOTHER: Scared mad of what? I've been through this eleven years. You don't even remember when we came here!

JIMMY: You're scared —'cause of the baby!

MOTHER: (*moves towards him, then stops uncertainly*) Bring the wood — and don't say another word!

JIMMY: Okay, Mom. (*Goes stage right door into another room. MOTHER stares down at her stomach and wrings her hands nervously. JIMMY reappears, carrying jacket and scarf.*)

MOTHER: Dress warm. Make sure to do up all the buttons. Let me help you . . .

JIMMY: I can do them myself. I'm no baby.

MOTHER: All right — all right. Jimmy . . . I'm sorry about what I said — about your father . . .

JIMMY: Can't be helped.

MOTHER: It ain't the truth, an' yet, it is. Jimmy — it ain't right for him to be away from us all the time.

JIMMY: He's doin' it for us — you said so yourself!

MOTHER: I know — he's doin' it for us. But sometimes, I don't want it. There's you . . . what about your school? You finish this year — you gotta go into town for high school. I'm gonna be here . . . myself.

JIMMY: I'm not goin' to no town school!

MOTHER: You're doin' as you're told, and that's it. Now get the wood.

JIMMY: One armload?

MOTHER: It will do. (*JIMMY opens door stage left and steps out. Gust of wind and mother wraps her garments around her shoulders.*) Jimmy.

JIMMY: (*offstage*) Yah.

MOTHER: Look if you can see the lights at Williams' place!

JIMMY: (*offstage*) Okay.

MOTHER: (*at window*) Wind, snow and night — I wish I was dead! (*suddenly, fearfully moves to the door and opens it*) Jimmy! Jimmy!

JIMMY: (*offstage*) Yah?

MOTHER: Don't go off the road! Stay near the house.

JIMMY: I'll go see if the snowplow's comin'.

MOTHER: No! you just come back here!

JIMMY: (*offstage*) Aw, okay . . .

MOTHER: (*to herself*) Fool kid — could get lost an' freeze to death.

JIMMY: (*enters with armload of wood, which he deposits noisily in woodbox*) Whew! It's cold out there! Must be about ten below . . .

MOTHER: I know — close the door. Did you see the light from the Williams' farm?

JIMMY: Heck no. You can't see nothin' out there.

MOTHER: Great — you can't see nothin' — can't hear nothin' — just this howling and snow. Not a telephone within

189

four miles of the house, an' no way to get out if we had to! Oh, damn this sort of life!

JIMMY: Why we need a telephone for? (*goes to cupboard and takes out checker board and checkers*)

MOTHER: To . . . to call someone if our house burns down, that's why!

JIMMY: (*startled*) Our house ain't gonna burn, is it, Mom?

MOTHER: No, it wouldn't burn. We could have worse things happen.

JIMMY: Like what?

MOTHER: Like nothin'.

JIMMY: (*laying out checker board*) Have you a game.

MOTHER: (*paces nervously*) Yeh . . .

JIMMY: You don't wanna play, do you?

MOTHER: (*savagely*) Sure I wanna play — I'm dyin' to play! Come on — lay the board out and let's get going!

JIMMY: Mom . . .

MOTHER: And don't tell me to take another aspirin — I've got aspirins right up to here (*runs finger across her throat*)

JIMMY: (*stops laying board and lowers his head sullenly*) Okay, Mom.

MOTHER: (*sitting down opposite him*) All right, let's play. You not playing? I'm sorry, son . . . What do you want me to do — smile like a hyena? I don't feel in the least happy — what kind of life is it for us, cooped up like two rats in a hole? It's . . . well, it's dangerous, an' I'm worried . . .

JIMMY: That's all right. Why you worried?

MOTHER: Anything can happen. One of us could get sick . . . or . . . or the baby could come during this storm! It could come anytime now . . .

JIMMY: It ain't gonna come!

MOTHER: Go tell that to whatever's above us.

JIMMY: No, Mom! You gotta make it so it don't come!

MOTHER: All right — maybe it won't come. We can wish, if you want. There's nothin' I can do to stop it, though. Let's have that game. (*reaches over and begins laying out board*) Your move . . . what you playing, reds or blacks?

JIMMY: I don't wanna play.

MOTHER: You just stay there and play, or I'm gonna give you a thick lip for your nonsense. (*boy moves with disinterest*)

JIMMY: Does Dad know — about the baby?

MOTHER: I'd be in a helluva fix if he didn't!

JIMMY: Huh!

MOTHER: Nothing. Your mom was being funny.

JIMMY: There's nothin' funny about dyin'!

MOTHER: Who's talkin' about dying'?

JIMMY: You're dyin'! Lots of mothers die having babies. Our teacher said so!

MOTHER: How many babies has your teacher had?

JIMMY: None. She ain't married yet. Ain't you even worried?

MOTHER: What worries I got ain't about dying, that's for sure. Here — keep your mind on your game. You've lost two checkers right there!

JIMMY: Okay. Why we have to have a baby?

MOTHER: Because — well, because we want a baby. It's gonna be for you as much as for your father an' me.

JIMMY: You ain't doin' it for me!

MOTHER: Now what kind of way is that to talk? You learn such bad manners in school? Must've — you ain't learned them at home! What you want me to do — cry for you?

JIMMY: You don't have to do nothin' for me . . .

MOTHER: Well then give us a little fun if you're that happy. You act like you was at a funeral.

JIMMY: (*making move*) You sure weren't watchin' that time!

MOTHER: (*rising and going to window*) I don't want to play no more. Why we got to get stuck in this god-forsaken hole I'll never know. Pinchin' coins — spendin' money in two places — never getting a decent crop off the fields — and then bein' trapped like this! This ain't livin' — it ain't even dyin' — just a sort of limbo in between. An' they killed Indians for this once — cripes!

JIMMY: You don't like the farm, Mom?

MOTHER: I hate the place, Jimmy. I hate it like I never thought I'd hate anything!

JIMMY: Then why we livin' here?

MOTHER: Because your father wants a kind of freedom that don't exist. (*turning to boy*) All his life he's worked underground, in the mines. For a long time after we married, we lived in small mining towns — in company houses where you spent days cleaning up the muck of the last family whose man got fired or layed off. After you was born, he got this urge of his — for a piece of land to call his own — someplace he could step on twice or three times a year and say this was all his . . .

JIMMY: It's all ours, too!

MOTHER: No, it ain't! It's his an' his alone. I don't want it — an' you can't afford to waste your life here after you finish school. It's gonna be the same with the baby, so what's this place worth to anybody? Nothin'! An' it's bleeding us dry. We can't even afford a telephone. Be nobody to call even if we had one. I don't know anybody anymore, except the Williams people — an' they're not much for socializing with — too busy making money with their cattle an' sheep.

JIMMY: I like it here — I want to live here!

MOTHER: That's a bunch of baloney! You'd kill yourself tryin' to make something of the farm. New buildings to put up — all the land to clear and cultivate — you don't even know where you'd have to begin!

JIMMY: But I like it!

MOTHER: Oh, sure — that makes it all just dandy! Your father likes it, too — just so long's he doesn't have to live here. Boy, we don't belong here — it's like night an' day between country an' city people. An' we ain't neither now.

JIMMY: We're farmers . . .

MOTHER: Farmers? Betcha Mrs. Williams is sitting pretty — baking her pies and roasts right now — she don't even hear the storm! Me? I'm scared of it — scared like everything was taken out of me and off me — leavin' me cold. You ever see the cemetary back of the church? That's where the Williams' are buried — an' the McFarlands, and Fedoras. That's where the claim to bein' farmers is made . . . not jus' wantin' to farm. You gotta live here all your life, an' then you gotta die. I'm town-born, an' you're too young to know what you want, an' that's why we don't belong.

JIMMY: That ain't so — people like us here. You an' Mrs. Williams are good friends.

MOTHER: (*laughs harshly*) When was the last time she visited us?

JIMMY: (*thinking*) I . . . I guess sometimes last summer.

MOTHER: When last summer?

JIMMY: The Sunday they came over with their new car.

MOTHER: An' we ain't even got a horse an' buggy to show off with. Put some water on for tea.

JIMMY rises, and finding a kettle, carries it to water bucket to fill it. A strong gust of wind is heard outside and the kitchen light dims and goes out.

JIMMY: Hey — Mom! What happened?

MOTHER: I dunno. Check the light in your room.

Sounds of boy stumbling out of kitchen, then returning.

JIMMY: It won't light!

MOTHER: The powerline is down, I guess. Just stay where you are. I'll light the lamp . . .

She withdraws oil lamp from cupboard and lights it.

JIMMY: It's kinda dark an' scarey, ain't it, Mom?

MOTHER: Well, you can always get ready for bed.

JIMMY: I don't want to sleep . . . Gee, listen to it blow! Do you think it could cover our house up?

MOTHER: It will blow itself out by morning.

JIMMY: Supposin' it don't. Supposin' it blows like this for a week?

195

MOTHER: It's not going to blow no week . . .

JIMMY: How do you know?

MOTHER: Read a book — do anything, but just leave me alone! (*prepares tea and takes down a loaf of bread*) You want a peanut-butter sandwich?

JIMMY: I don't know . . .

MOTHER: Well, do you, or don't you? I'm not waiting all night for you to make up your mind!

JIMMY: (*nods*) Yes, I do. (*she cuts bread angrily*) Mom — how much does a television set cost?

MOTHER: Why you askin'?

JIMMY: Just wanted to know . . .

MOTHER: Now you want a fancy television set in the house, I suppose!

JIMMY: No — I was just askin' . . .

MOTHER: You know how far we're behind with our payments on the farm?

JIMMY: I . . . was just askin' . . .

MOTHER: We ain't paid a payment since September . . . now what you think of that?

JIMMY: (*rising*) I don't wanna talk about it.

MOTHER: Where you going?

JIMMY: I'm going to bed. We don't ever have any fun no more.

MOTHER: Jimmy . . . look at me . . . see how . . . here . . . look at my hands. See how blue and hard the veins stand out — like those of an old person. Jimmy — I'm only thirty-four years old! I'm young yet! I wanna live and laugh as much as you! Jimmy, I'm sorry!

JIMMY: (*turning away*) Goodnight, Mom.

MOTHER: (*Watches him leave room. Bewildered, she runs her hand over her face and brushes her hair back.*) Goodnight, Son. (*Starts to cut bread aimlessly. Suddenly she shudders with pain, and dropping knife to floor, grips edge of the counter.*) Jimmy!

JIMMY: (*re-enters kitchen, dressed only in trousers*) What's wrong, Mom?

MOTHER: The baby, Jimmy . . . The baby is coming soon!

JIMMY: (*frightened*) What you saying, Mom?

MOTHER: Damnit! Where's the light? Where's the snow plow?

JIMMY: You not goin' to have the baby now?

MOTHER: No — not this minute! Jimmy — listen to me — could you go over to Mrs. Williams — ask her to come here right away?

JIMMY: It's four miles, Mom. There's no road — no way of seein' . . .

MOTHER: Are you scared to go?

JIMMY: I can try if you want me to.

MOTHER: Get your clothes on. (*JIMMY leaves room and mother walks painfully over to the window. Scratches vengefully at the ice on the pane.*) No light . . . no friends — what's he want me to do? Bust my brains out! Jim — come here!

JIMMY: (*comes in, buttoning his sleeves and carrying scarf in hand*) I'll hurry!

MOTHER: It's no use, boy — you won't see your nose out there!

JIMMY: I'll go.

MOTHER: What — an' get lost an' freeze to death! I got enough problems without that . . . What can I do . . . What can I do?

JIMMY: How long — before the baby comes?

MOTHER: I don't know. An hour maybe — maybe six hours. I'll know when it hurts next time.

JIMMY: Maybe the snowplow will come an' Dad will get here . . .

MOTHER: Sure — we'll just hold our breath an' wait!

JIMMY: Why don't you go to bed, Mom?

MOTHER: There's time. There's a time to live, an' a time to die. We ain't done much livin', you an' I, boy.

JIMMY: Mom — don't say that!

MOTHER: A body's got to talk, or we'd choke on the stuff that's in us. I'm not a mother — never been much of a mother to you.

JIMMY: You're all right — you're a good mom . . .

MOTHER: See your sock. Your big toe's been out of that sock two weeks now. I've known it all along, but never took it off to mend it. That's the kind of mother I am, Jimmy. Same with helping you out in homework — not that I could help. Never went past grade six myself. Figured I knew everything there was to know. I was more of a kid than you are now when I got marrried. I can tear things apart, but I can't build nothin', Jimmy.

JIMMY: If you want, I'll take the lamp in, an' straighten out your bed.

MOTHER: I said all them sore things about your father. It was only me talkin', Son. Him an' I both did our share to bust life up. He don't want to come home now . . .

JIMMY: He does too — you're jus' sayin' that!

MOTHER: When he was home last spring . . . we talked of divorce.

JIMMY: No!

MOTHER: (*fiercely*) Oh yes! Only thing holding us back then

199

was it would cost too much. It's all right now — there's the baby an' the cost — an' that's got your father an' me licked good! So don't worry.

JIMMY: The baby — who's gonna help you? You can't have the baby by yourself, can you?

MOTHER: (*shrugs weakly*) I dunno — you're gonna help, I guess . . .

JIMMY: I won't!

MOTHER: You haven't much choice. Either that, or goin' out there an' gettin' yourself lost.

JIMMY: I'm gonna go get Mrs. Williams.

MOTHER: No you're not. Besides, what makes you think dear Mrs. Williams would risk coming out an' gettin' her feet cold tonight — baby or no baby?

JIMMY: I'm goin' anyway!

MOTHER: (*turning on him with animal ferocity*) You're stayin' right here — or I'm gonna wipe the floor with you! You hear me?

Defeated, JIMMY sits in chair and, burying his head in his arms, begins to cry.

MOTHER: (*walks toward JIMMY softly*) Jimmy — don't do that . . . I never seen you cry since you was short enough to walk under this table! Don't do that . . . Tell you what — I'll make us both peanut-butter sandwiches, an' we'll have a big pot of tea after — jus' the two of us. That be nice? (*takes JIMMY's shoulders between her hands*)

JIMMY: (*still weeping*) Leave me alone!

MOTHER: Don't cry, Jimmy — it'll all be different after this. We'll move. Soon's your father comes, we'll tell him we want to go back with him. If he don't like the idea, we'll go back anyway. There'll be television for you, an' good schools an' work when you get older. An' there'll be people an' places to go at night for your father an' me. We'll have a good life — an' even if we don't have money, we'll be able to laugh again.

JIMMY: I'm happy . . .

MOTHER: You never been happy — your father an' I seen to that. We never give you a childhood, an' what little you had — I'm gonna take away from you tonight. Jimmy — kiss your mama . . .

Kitchen light flickers and comes on.

JIMMY: (*raising his head*) What happened?

MOTHER: They fixed the powerline — that's what happened! We got light again an' that's more love than a human heart got! (*She releases JIMMY's shoulders and, picking up the knife, busies herself with preparing food*)

JIMMY: (*staring at her*) You didn't mean it, did you Mom? You didn't wait . . .

MOTHER: Wait for what?

JIMMY: Me to kiss you.

MOTHER: (*brings platter of sandwiches and pot of tea to table*) Bring us some cups.

JIMMY: (*getting cups*) You really meant it, Mom?

MOTHER: (*cringes with another pain*) Yes . . . yes, I meant it! Somehow, I never learned to say things the way I want to say them to you.

JIMMY: You gonna say them to the baby?

MOTHER: Yes, I will!

JIMMY: Mom — you ain't gonna get terrible sick — you ain't gonna die or something?

MOTHER: No, Jimmy! Baby's gonna be born real easy — you gotta help me five, ten minutes — I'll tell you what to do. After that, it'll be all right. By morning, baby'll be sleeping an' I'll get up and work like any other morning. Snowplow will come, an' your dad will be home — an' we'll all have a big laugh about it!

JIMMY: You'll love me, wontcha, Mom?

MOTHER: You askin' me? You ought to be ashamed of yourself!

JIMMY: I . . . I'm sorry for askin' . . .

MOTHER: Take the lamp into my room — just in case the power goes off again. An' while you're there, look in the linen cupboard. Take out all the towels you can find, an' put them by my pillow. Also, an extra blanket.

JIMMY: It ain't gonna happen soon, is it, Mom?

MOTHER: Yes — very soon.

JIMMY: I'm scared!

MOTHER: (*harshly*) I don't care what you feel — do as you're told! (*Boy takes lamp and leaves kitchen. MOTHER fills kettle full and places it on stove, then walks to window. But instead of peering out, she rubs her hands over her face wearily.*) Why don't he run? Why don't he kick my face in? Whose kid is he? He ain't me, an' he ain't him . . . He . . . he cried . . . an' then he wanted to kiss me. God! I got no right doin' this to him!

JIMMY: (*re-entering kitchen*) I only found three towels.

MOTHER: That's enough. I'll need some strong string an' a pair of scissors, then you can go to bed. I'll call you.

JIMMY: I don't feel sleepy. Mom — is it gonna hurt you or the baby?

MOTHER: Suppose babies don't like gettin' born — but that's his worry.

JIMMY: And you?

MOTHER: No, it ain't gonna hurt . . .

JIMMY: Then what you need me for?

MOTHER: To wipe its mouth an' make it cry!

JIMMY: Why?

MOTHER: *(turning on him suddenly)* Because that's the way it all begins — you wipe its mouth an' make it cry — AN' IT'S GONNA LIVE — THAT'S WHY!

Curtain

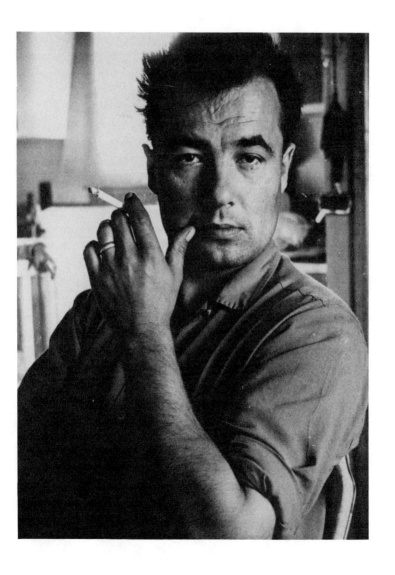

GEORGE RYGA:
A SELECTED CHRONOLOGY

1949

"Smoke" (essay)*

1950

"The Stray" (poem)

1954

"Federico García Lorca" (poem)

1956

Song of My Hands (poetry)

1958

"Prairie Wind" (poem)

1959

"New Days" (poem)
"The Last Visit" (poem unpublished)
"What's it in Need of?" (poem unpublished)
These Songs I Sing (poetry)

1960

"The Bridge" (novel, unpublished)*
"Heritage" (novella, unpublished)
"High Noon and Long Shadows" (short story)
"Gold in the Aspens" (short story)*
"The Wife of Sid Malan" (short story)
"The Meek Shall Inherit (short story, written under
   pseudonym Elgin Troy)*
Night Desk (novel)

1961

"A Touch of Cruelty" (short story)
"Betrothal" (short story)
"Golden Boy" (short story, manuscript lost)
"Glow Worm on the Beach" (short story, manuscript lost)
"Businessman's Dilemma" (short story, manuscript lost)
"Pinetree Ghetto" (short story)
"Wagoner Lad" (novel, manuscript lost)
"Village Crossroad" (television drama)*
"A Touch of Cruelty" (television drama)
"Gold in the Aspens" (television drama)

1962

"Love by Parcel Post" (short story)*
"Nellie-Boy" (short story)*
"Half-Caste" (short story)*
"Brothers" (short story)
"Legacy of the Meek (short story)
"Recollections of a Stone-Picker" (novel)
"Indian" (television drama, adaptation of "Pinetree Ghetto")
"Storm" (stage and/or television drama)*
"Trouble in Mind" (television drama)
"Recollections of a Stone-Picker (previously titled "A Forever
 Kid," radio drama)
"Poor People" (short story collection, unpublished)

1963

Hungry Hills (novel, written 1960)
"Thy Sawdust Temples" (novel, manuscript lost)
"Old Sam" (novel, manuscript lost)
"Indian" (radio drama)
"Country Boy" (short story for radio)
"Men of the Mountain" (novella, unpublished)
"Two Soldiers" (television drama)

"Bitter Grass" (television drama)

"Chelkash" (television drama)

"For Want of Something Better to Do" (television drama, adapted from Gorky)

"The Tulip Garden" (television drama)

"The Pear Tree" (television drama)

"Goodbye is for Keeps" (television drama)

"Masks and Shadows" (television drama)

"Bread Route" (television drama)

"Departures" (radio drama)

"Ballad for Bill" (radio drama)

1964

"The Stone Angel" (radio drama, adapted from a Margaret Lawrence novel)

"Poor Boy" (television drama, adaptation of *Hungry Hills*)

"Indian" (stage play)

"Moderato Cantabile" (television drama, adapted from a Marguerite Duras novel)

"Why Rock the Boat" (television drama, adapted from a William Weintraub novel)

"A White Dog on a Green Lawn" (television drama)

"The Hungry Hills" (television drama)

1965

"The Third Day of Summer" (novel, unfinished, unpublished)

"Fallen Angels" (novel, unfinished, unpublished)

"Profiles in Dust" (short story, unpublished)

"The Grey Side of the Mountain" (television drama)

"Heritage" (novel, unpublished)

"A Feast of Thunder" (novella, unpublished)

"The Kamloops Incident" (television documentary drama)

"Heritage" (television drama)

"Man Alive" (television drama)

"A Feast of Thunder" (television drama)
"Men of the Mountain" (radio drama)

1966

"Valley of the Stars" (abstract for a novel, unpublished)
Ballad of A Stone-Picker (novel)
"Man Alive" (novel, unpublished)
"Nothing But a Man" (stage play)
"The White Transparent" (television drama)
"The Jingle-Jangle Children" (television drama)
"Child Under a Leaf" (screenplay)

1967

"The Napkin" (television drama)
"Pretty World" (television drama)
The Ecstasy of Rita Joe (stage play)
"Notes From A Silent Boyhood" (autobiographical essay)*
"Black is the Color" (short story)
"The Kamloops Incident" (screenplay)
"A Builder in Stone, A Builder in Wood" (screenplay)
"A Carpenter by Trade" (television documentary)
"Pray for us Sinners" (television drama)
"Just an Ordinary Person" (television drama, adapted from
  Gorky)

1968

"The Maze" (television drama)
"No Secrets" (television drama)
"Half-Way House" (television drama)
"Just an Ordinary Person" (stage play, adapted from Gorky)
"Long Morning of a Short Day" (television drama)
"Halfway to Neverland" (television drama)
"There Are No Secrets In My Court" (television drama)

"The Manipulators" (two scripts for a television series)
"Grass and Wild Strawberries" (stage play)

1969

"Compressions" (stage play)
"Contemporary Theatre and its Language" (essay)

1970

"A Question of Survival" (television drama)
"Captives of a Faceless Drummer" (stage play)
"The Bionic Woman" (television drama)

1971

"A Feast of Thunder" (oratorio)
"The Ecstasy of Rita Joe" (screenplay)
"Riders of the Dunes" (screenplay)
"Betrothal" (television drama)
"The Overlanders" (television drama)
"Ninth Summer" (television drama)
Captives of the Faceless Drummer (stage play)

1972

"The Lately Wind Has Ceased" (poem)
"Captives of the Faceless Drummer" (radio drama)
"In Search of the Nightingale" (radio drama)
Sunrise on Sarah (stage play)
"Ballad of A Muskrat" (screenplay)
"A Child in a Prison Camp" (screenplay)
"Paracelsus" (stage play)

1973

"Portrait of Angelica" (stage play)
"The Sparrow's Fall" (screenplay)

"The Rocky Mountains" (television documentary)
"Sunrise on Sarah" (television drama)
"Miners, Gentlemen and Other Hard Cases" (12-episode radio series)

1974

"Theatre in Canada" (essay)
"Melina Mercouri Eating an Orange" (poem)
"The Odyssey of Herbie Johnson" (screenplay)
"Glory Ride" (screenplay)

1975

"The Ballad of Ivan Lepa" (television drama)
"Seasons of a Summer Day" (radio drama)

1976

"Advocates of Danger" (10-episode radio series)
Night Desk (novel)
"The Last of the Gladiators" (stage play)
Seven Hours to Sundown (stage play)
Ploughmen of the Glacier (stage play)
"Rider on a Galloping Horse" (essay)

1977

"Tuesday Morning" (poem)
"Echo from a Distant Field" (radio drama)
"How Do I Love Thee" (radio drama)
"A New Land" (television drama — "Newcomer" series)
"Ploughmen of the Glacier" (radio drama)
"The Need for Mythology" (essay)

1978

"Visit from the Pension Lady" (short story)

"Mike's Song" (poem)
"Jeremiah's Place" (stage play)
"Prometheus Bound" (stage play, adaptation of *Aeschylus*)

1979

"The Ragged Conquerors" (novel fragment)
Beyond the Crimson Morning (travel memoir)

1980

"Twelve Ravens for the Sun" (oratorio, Ryga/Theodorakis collaboration)
"The Winds of Saturn" (screenplay)
"A Voyage of the Damned (novel, unfinished)

1981

A Letter to My Son (stage drama)
"One Sad Song for Henry" (radio drama)
"Seven Hours to Sundown" (radio drama)
"The Romeo Kuchmir Story" (stage adaptation of *Night Desk*)
"Captives of the Faceless Drummer" (radio drama)

1982

"Paracelsus" (radio drama)
"A Letter to My Son" (radio drama)
"The Artist in Resistance" (essay)

1983

"The Bells of Grenada" (radio drama)
"The Landscape and the Legend" (poetry)
"The Star" (short story, unpublished)
"The Gray Mountains of Cosala" (short story, unpublished)

1984

"Visions of Theatre in America" (essay)
"The Addict" (radio drama)
"The Grey Lady of Rupert Street" (short story, unpublished)
"Old Charlie" (radio drama)
"Mist from the Mountain" (short story, unpublished)

1985

"A Portrait of Angelica" (radio drama)
"One More for the Road" (stage play)
"Essay on *A Letter to My Son*" (essay)*
In the Shadow of the Vulture (novel, written 1981)

1986

"A Love Story" (short story, unpublished)
"Crash Landing" (short story, unpublished)
"Hospitality People" (short story, unpublished)
"The Village of Melons" (revised short story)
"Angel" (short story, unpublished)
"The Children of Moses" (stage play, unpublished)
"Glaciers in the Sun" (stage musical drama)
"Brendon Willie and the Great Event" (radio drama)

1987

"Dear Yousef" (short story, unpublished)
"Rabbit Farm" (short story, unpublished)
"A Kind of Graffiti" (short story, unpublished)
"Diary of a Foolish Man" (short story, unpublished)
"The Private Obsessions of Andrew, the Waiter" (short story, unpublished)
"When Music Was First Heard" (short story, unpublished)
"East-West Politics and Cultural Influences" (essay)
"Resurrection" (poem)

Undated Material

"The Lake on Blue Mountain" (television drama)
"The Wind Rider" (television drama)
"The High Tower" (television drama)
"Point of Danger" (television drama)
"One October Evening" (short story fragment)*
"The Apartment" (short story, unpublished)
"Diary of a Small Person" (short story, unpublished)
"Replies to A Questionnaire" (for Zoë Cope)
"Maria — Weekly Song June 20th" (poem, unpublished)

* *appears in this publication*

Bibliography of Main Works by George Ryga

Song of My Hands, Edmonton, Alberta: Ryga, 1956
These Songs I Sing, Wales, U.K.: Publisher unknown, 1959
Hungry Hills, Toronto, Ontario: Longmans, 1963
Hungry Hills, London, England: Michael Joseph, 1965
Ballad of A Stone-Picker, Toronto, Ontario: MacMillan, 1966
Ballad of A Stone-Picker, London, England: Michael Joseph, 1966
Indian, Agincourt, Ontario: Book Society, 1968
The Ecstasy of Rita Joe, Vancouver, B.C.: Talonbooks, 1970
The Ecstay of Rita Joe and Other Plays, Toronto, Ontario: New Press, 1971
Captives of the Faceless Drummer, Vancouver, B.C.: Talonbooks, 1971
Sunrise on Sarah, Vancouver, B.C.: Talonbooks, 1973
Hungry Hills, Vancouver, B.C.: Talonbooks, 1974
Ballad of A Stonepicker, Vancouver, B.C.: Talonbooks, 1976
Night Desk, Vancouver, B.C.: Talonbooks, 1976
Seven Hours to Sundown, Vancouver, B.C.: Talonbooks, 1977
Ploughmen of the Glacier, Vancouver, B.C.: Talonbooks, 1977

Beyond the Crimson Morning, Garden City, N.Y.: Doubleday, 1979

Two Plays: Paracelsus and Prometheus Bound, Winnipeg, Man.: Turnstone, 1982

A Portrait of Angelica/A Letter to My Son, Winnipeg, Man.: Turnstone, 1984

In the Shadow of the Vulture, Vancouver, B.C.: Talonbooks, 1985

In the Shadow of the Vulture, Kiev, U.S.S.R.: *Vsesvit* Magazine, 1988

In the Shadow of the Vulture, Kiev, U.S.S.R.: Dnipro, 1988

Resurrection, Kiev, U.S.S.R.: *Vsesvit* Magazine, 1988

The Athabasca Ryga, Vancouver, B.C.: Talonbooks, 1990